IRON

ANTIQUE BITS, SPURS AND STIRRUPS
FROM THE NEVZOROV HAUTE ÉCOLE COLLECTION

IRON
ANTIQUE BITS, SPURS AND STIRRUPS
FROM THE NEVZOROV HAUTE ÉCOLE COLLECTION

Copyright © 2012 by Alexander Nevzorov
Photographs © Lydia Nevzorova
Published by Nevzorov Haute École

www.hauteecole.ru

All rights reserved.

Printed in Charleston, S.C., United States of America.
No part of this book may be used or reproduced in any manner whatsoever without written permission except in the case of brief quotations embodied in critical articles and reviews.

ISBN 13: 978-5-904788-17-9

Photos 3.10, 4.4, 4.5 provided by Marie Duizidou,
Nevzorov Haute École Student

Photo on page 34 provided by Sophia Spartantseva,
Nevzorov Haute École Student

Project Head: Lydia Nevzorova
Managing Editor: Donna Condrey-Miller
Production Manager and Editor: Stasya Zolotova
Editorial Staff : Varvara Lyubovnaya, Cloe Lacroix, Marie Duizidou
Art Director: Dmitri Raikin
Head of Pre-press Department: Eugene Mushtay

PREFACE

Cavemen only hunted horses for their meat, skin and bones. During this period horses were then only the size of a small pony.

The earliest evidence of the domestication of the horse dates from the second half of the fourth millennium B.C. in the south of the Ukraine. In Mesopotamia, we find that in the first third of the third millennium B.C. the horse is used as a means of traction for chariots. We see this on a Sumerian tablet known as The Standard of Ur, dated 2700 B.C., from the royal cemetery of the old city of Ur. This tablet is on display in the British Museum in London. These people had certainly realized the power of the animal and the superiority a chariot brought to the warrior, thanks to its speed and its maneuverability. However, if the proportions of the horses and the warrior are depicted correctly, a rider placed on horseback would see his feet dragging along the floor.

Assyrian cavalry, with riders on horseback, appear for the first time during the ninth century B.C., and the representation of riders show us that the size of the horse has increased. On this stele, we notice that the Assyrian warrior rides his horse without stirrups as they were not introduced into this part of country until the seventh century A.D. Consequently, he has to jump onto his horse.

When man understood that the power and speed of the horse could make him superior in the face of his opponents, it became necessary to invent an item allowing him to transmit his orders to his horse. Man had noticed that, in the mouth of the animal, there was a place without teeth, but particularly sensitive, now called the bars. It is there that the genius of man decided to place a small metallic bar connected to the reins. The bit was born!

The bit, called "frenum" by Romans, is similar to the steering wheel and the brake pedal of a car. Dressage and Equestrian Art were still in their early stages and to obtain an immediate submission of the horse people invented bits as real instruments of torture with sharp edges or points on the mouthpiece.

This barbaric horse riding continued until the 18th century when riders developed a method of riding in which the obedience of the animal would be obtained by less cruel methods. Thus Equestrian Art was born and famous riding instructors began to pass their knowledge to their pupils. However, it is a pity nothing has ever prevented man from being cruel to animals in every period, sometimes through pride but very often through ignorance.

The magnificent work of Lydia and Alexander Nevzorov presents us with pieces of harness, bits, stirrups, and spurs, of exceptional quality which are a reflection of the importance of the people to whom they belonged. Some of the luxurious items are unique pieces, not constrained by the classical model of the period but reflecting the wish of their owners to distinguish themselves from their contemporaries.

The greatest credit goes to these two authors who have gathered these beautiful pieces in a sumptuous book, illustrated with magnificent photographs. We warmly congratulate them on their initiative. This book will take an important place in the libraries of both equestrians and lovers of fine books.

The authors offer those, such as me, who have no possibility of seeing these pieces in life, the opportunity to appreciate the great quality of the wonderful items shown throughout this book.

Pierre Drugmand
President CIDE
Club International d'Eperonnerie

* * *

NHE publishing is very grateful to *Pierre M. Desclos* and *Pierre Drugmand* for their help in attributation of items presented in the book.

INTRODUCTION

The history of equine iron, that is, of snaffles, curb bits, spurs and stirrups cannot be examined and understood except in the context of the very dramatic history of the relationship between man and horse. A history of the iron in and of itself would not be very well understood and would, most likely, be terribly boring. In any event, it is not important whether the chomping abrasions on Scythian snaffles were being induced or what the curvature of the cheek pieces of Greek or Persian curb bits was, but rather, the fact of how this iron worked and that it transformed the relationship of horse and man into an eternal problem.

The iron of every era is fantastically informative.

Iron in general, is very truthful, very direct and straightforward.

The masters of bas-relief, painters, and men of letters can lie artistically as much as they like and however they like about the relationship of man and horse and they can create a certain romantic illusion, but by looking closely at the iron of one era or another, the truth becomes clear.

It becomes clear what kind of relationship it really was, what man wanted, what the horse did not want, what riding was like and how great or worthless was the rider's skill.

Using the truest imagery, I want it to be as clear for you as it is for me when I go over the innumerable snaffles, curb bits, spurs and stirrups of all eras, from the times of the Lurs to the Napoleonic days.

In each piece of iron — and the cruelty of the designs is staggering — is a breathtaking quantity of information about riding styles, about the characteristics of the horses, about the ambitions and customs of the era, about the peculiarities of war, and about human stupidity and the horse's pain.

Generally, it all was very much the same everywhere.

Whether in ancient Scythia, Assyria, or the Kingdom of the Lurs; whether in Rome, Egypt, or in the ancient caverns of the Celtic smiths; or beneath the piercingly white full-spectrum bright-as-daylight lamps in the workshops of modern England and Germany — over a period of almost 3,000 years the same exact activity has been and still is taking place, namely, the manufacture of metal contraptions, pieces of metal with differing forms which give man the illusion of authority over the very free, very strong and very defenseless horse.

From the moment man first understood that it is only through the infliction of pain could he force a horse to bear him on her back, he has contrived and concocted unbelievable contraptions, first trying to lessen the pain, then driving that pain to the limit.

The iron has become, for man, some kind of indispensable attribute of the relationship, a magical key for control of the horse…

1.1. Simple snaffle bits typical to all times and places. Nothing has changed up through the present.
Rus, 10th century; India, 10th century; Alans, 10th century; Mongolia, 13th century

CHAPTER 1
BITS

There is a great illusion which consists of the point that man controls the horse in sports, in front of the cart and in the cavalry. That is not true.

Pain controls the horse.

They stop the horse with pain, they direct her with pain and they turn her with pain.

As a matter of fact, the whole history of riding is a history of equine pain.

And it all began very simply, with a small ring. Many thousands of years ago, wishing to control the horse, man used a ring which was driven into the skin and cartilage horse's nostrils, breaking the nasal septum.

Who was the first to think of this stupidity?

Sumerian images (2500 B.C.) have been preserved in which this ring in the horse's nose is clearly visible.

This is evidence only that the Sumerians knew how and loved to draw, and not that they were the first or second to do this, and not that other peoples did not practice this method. One way or the other, whoever it was, it gave rise to something bad.

Thanks to the Sumerian picture, it is easy to imagine the technology for installing the ring.

A bronze ring was driven into the nostrils, into the nasal septum, breaking through it, and then it was clamped.

One or two cords were tied to it, and the rider was able crudely and roughly control the horse while sitting on her or while standing in a cart or chariot attached.

The method was absolutely impractical.

First, there was great difficulty in the installation of such a ring. There were no tranquilizers, and the ability to lay down a horse quickly, accurately and without any gadgets was still unknown, so the horse had to be thrown down by ten people and her legs bound. The procedure itself of hammering the ring was sickening (owing to the clamping of the ring or the connecting of it, if the ring was wooden) and rather difficult.

Antibiotics, of course, were unknown, the bronze and wooden rings were responsible for the acute inflammation, necrosis and the break down of the very thin nasal septum was often a result.

Then man began to seek out in the horse a somewhat simpler, albeit just as vulnerable, tender and sensitive place from which he could gain control.

He found this place — it turned out to be the mouth.

And that is when the so-called "equine iron" was invented.

In the 2,500 years that passed from the time of the creation of the Sumerian picture "with the rings," humans have invented an astonishingly long list of devices for use in the horse's mouth.

The principle always remained about the same, but the degree of cruelty varied. A horse's iron, roughly speaking, is divided into two categories — "trigeminal" action (when the branches of the trigeminus nerve, which pass

1.2. Parthia
4th century B.C. Bronze, found in the Black Sea region

1.3. Parthia
4th century B.C.

1.4. Sarmatia
1st century B.C.

1.5. Central Russia
8th–9th centuries

1.6. Central Russia
4th–6th centuries

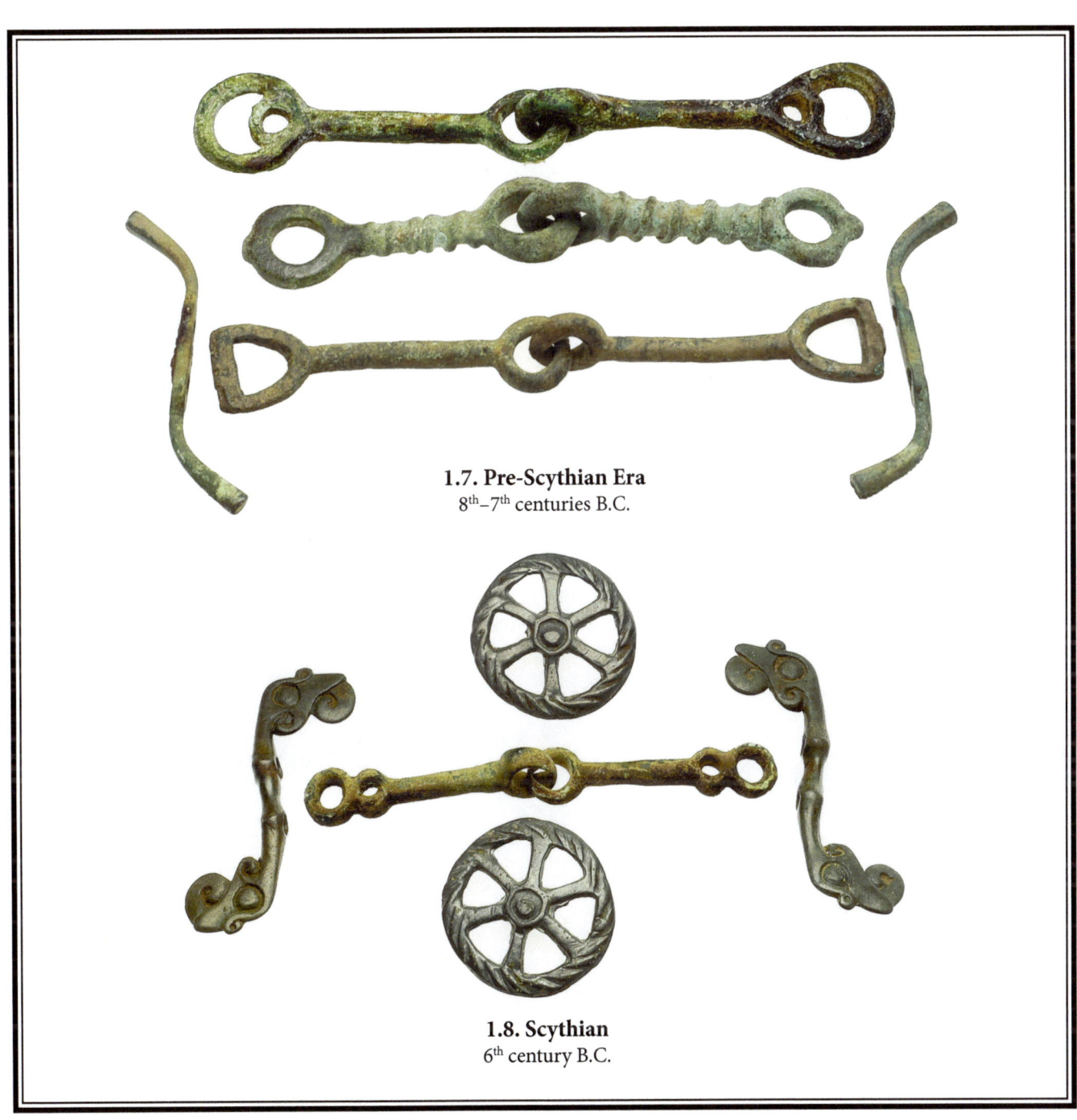

1.7. Pre-Scythian Era
8th–7th centuries B.C.

1.8. Scythian
6th century B.C.

1.9. Cimmerian
7th century B.C.

1.10. Antes
1st century

1.11. Scythian
4th century B.C.

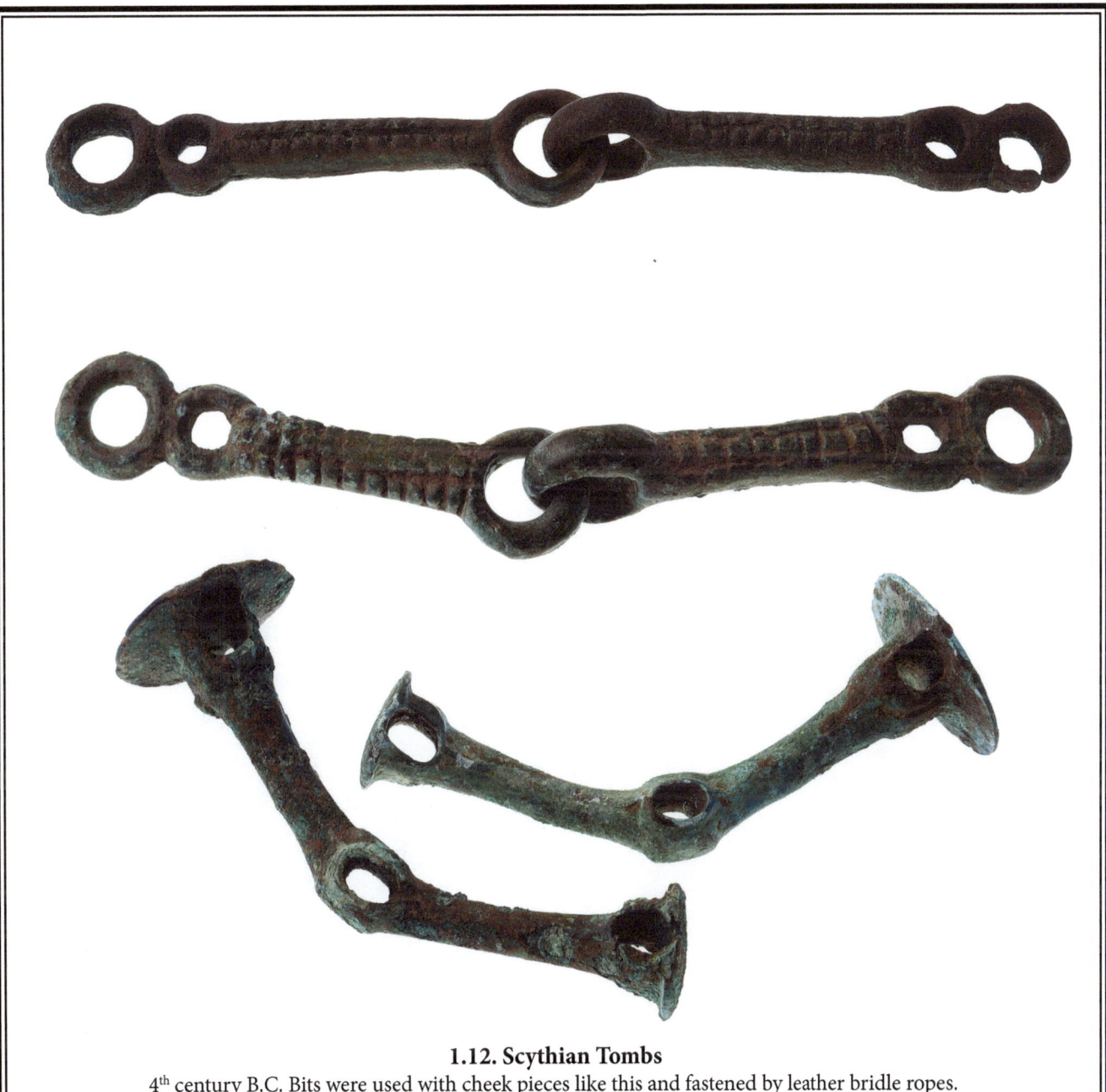

1.12. Scythian Tombs
4th century B.C. Bits were used with cheek pieces like this and fastened by leather bridle ropes.

1.13. Scythian bridle elements — cheek pieces and buckles
5th–3rd centuries B.C. Cheek pieces were fastened to the bit by leather ropes.

along the bones of the horse's lower jaw, are chosen as the main point of pain-infliction) and "dental" effect, where the very tender toothless areas — the bars, the teeth (first and second premolars), tongue, palate and gums are subjected to a direct painful influence — that is, direct pressure which acts upon nerves.

Trigeminal action iron is based more on intimidation. The horse, being a phenomenally intelligent creature, always will remember what kind of "mine" was put into her mouth by man. Such iron causes not a steady, cruel pain, but inflicts only one-time, short "injections" of this pain into the horse's brain and consciousness.

The Scythians, Cimmerians, Sarmats, Huns, Alans, Antes, Sogdians — almost all of the ancient world — used dental effect iron. It fully assured control at swift gaits, stopping, backing up as well as submission to primitive turns on one hind leg — the kind which are practiced today in circuses, where they are called "spins" — but nothing more than that.

Dental effect iron assumes constant usage of the rein, what now is called by the amusing phrase "contact with the mouth" — that is, these bits constantly remind the horse of her place and her servitude by inflicting continuous pain and discomfort.

It is difficult to say which type, the trigeminal or the dental, is more cruel.

I believe that they are approximately equal in cruelty.

Any trigeminal iron provides a direct painful impact on the minor palatine nerve, the branches of the maxillary nerve, the sublingual, the lingual and the branches of the trigeminus nerve.

Any dental iron provides a direct painful impact to the minor palatine nerve, the branches of the maxillary nerve, the sublingual and lingual nerves and the alveolar and infraorbital nerves.

This is a dry anatomical fact. There's no way around it.

* * *

Very pure iron existed as far back as Persia and Greece, in the Scythian and Cimmerian worlds and with the Sarmatian cavalry and the Huns.

There were the Scythian snaffle bits with the so-called "barbed cheek pieces" (see photo 1.14), which, at a pull of the rein on the required side, deeply pricked the horse's lips, facilitating for the Scythian rider a turn of the horse's head in the necessary direction and, accordingly, the rest of the equine body as well.

The fashion of the "barbed cheek pieces" stayed in vogue for all of the 4th century B.C. It is noteworthy that the sharpening of the twin barbs on all four shanks of the cheek pieces was so thorough that even now, after having lain 2,400 years in a Scythian chief's burial place, it can cause a finger to bleed at the lightest touch.

One can judge much based on Scythian bits with the barbed cheek pieces and on the first premolars of Scythian horses from the Pazyryk burrow that now repose in the halls of the Hermitage in St. Petersburg.

I had an occasion to examine them, and there, where I succeeded in turning back the skin of the lips which had been stiffening for 2,500 years, I looked closely at the teeth.

The teeth of riding horses were so wrecked by the iron (characteristic injuries, make no mistake) that everything about Scythian style of riding was immediately clear, and

1.14. Scytho-Meotian period, with barbed cheek pieces
4th century B.C.

it wasn't necessary to trouble myself searching for ancient training methods of Scythian horses.

Incidentally, they don't exist.

The only thing that is known is that the Scythians were the first who began breaking a young horse with lavish bloodletting. They calmly emptied about five liters of blood and then broke it, usually without any special drama and problems, since the great loss of blood weakened the horse and suppressed its craving to resist. They broke it at the time of the last snow, that is when it was completely exhausted by winter's hunger and immediately after agonizing castration. (The Scythians castrated their horses by smashing the testicles with special hammers).

Those remains of the Pazyryk horses are evidence that even foals were saddled for actual heavy work and for war: the joints, spine, and bones have the characteristic pathological changes which are particular to horses that were burdened blatantly from infancy when the skeleton still was not fully formed.

I have preserved Scythian foal bits from the third century B.C., which were found in one of the Crimean graves together with the bones of a foal. They are 6.5 centimeters wide, whereas the standard width of an adult's Scythian iron is 13 to 13.5 centimeters.

Lurians. Luristan is an area in southwest Iran. In ancient times it was famous for bronze working. Several Luristan bits of the 12th century B.C. remain. The main characteristic

1.15. Assyrian
4th century B.C. Even being rotten the spikes on the inner side of the cheek pieces may injure one's hands.

1.16. Unknown origin, possibly Tibet
Possibly 5th–10th centuries. Iron, silver.

1.17. Persian
3rd–5th centuries B.C.

of them are sophisticated, raised, one figured or multi figured cheek pieces. One variation can be seen in photo 1.18.

The Persians also left very conspicuous iron.

In figure 1.17 above, we see a very typical exhibit illustrating a kind of unity in the ancient world, in particular, the integration of the Persian culture into Greek civilization. Made of bronze and weighing 488 grams, there are 70 raised studs on the mouthpiece. The disks are absent. No one has been able to give a clear answer to the question of whether the bit was used for a riding horse or a driving horse, as the matter has not yet been investigated. Yet, despite some design similarities, the mouthpiece looks to be more of an Asian style. It reminds one of the Scythian mouthpieces of the period and at the same time the Chinese ones which would slightly favor the claims for its use on a riding horse.

1.18. Lurian bit with cheek piece figures
8th–7th centuries B.C.

1.19. Greek
3rd–5th centuries B.C.

One should bear in mind that the Scythian passion for freedom is purely a fictional cliché. In crude reality Herodotus mentioned some of the Scythian tribes as being a part of the Persian army during the military campaign against Hellas that was led by Xerxes, and during the Marathon battle and the battle at the Pass of Thermopylae and Plataea. The Scythians mentioned had been drafted to fight; they were not mercenary soldiers.

Greece and Rome.

The Greek curb bits of Athenian and Spartan types are very cruel devices with thorns. A mask of bronze bands was put onto the horse along with such a curb bit and the fine hooks on the cheek pieces played the role of fastening it as a unit to the mask.

Snaffle mouthpieces, meaning, the parts that are directly inside the horse's mouth, are not the only abomination with which horses were burdened. There were also the rings that cut the gums, and spikes and ripples, and a special screw to increase the painful effect.

In the photo 1.19 one can see a curb bit of bronze with a sophisticated combination of metals, some distinct iron stains can be seen all over the bit. The patina is of very light colour without malachite. The mouthpiece is adorned with 32 raised studs and palate-cutting discs, which were characteristic of the ancient world. Weight — 930 grams.

The ancient Greeks had an ideologue of early horsemanship, Xenophon, a very wise and gentle tutor to the horse, whom all of ancient Greece did not heed. Having abandoned in military and civilian use the famous spiked iron and awful masks, they increased the action of the iron and the fashion of horses. Unfortunately, this appliance was widely used in the time of Xenophon.

Of course, the term "curb" is used as a stretch of the definition and has been used in this context for the convenience of simplifying the terminology. In essence, it is the result of ordinary bit and cheek piece evolution into a single, rigidly fixed design whose effect is multiplied by pressure on the nasal bone produced by the upper part of the long shank.

Whenever the rider pulled the reins they would tighten and clench on the nose. (This fact was verified by tests on a model.) The mouthpiece and cheek pieces were designed with hooks (icheni), which probably served to attach the instrument to a bronze mask. Nevertheless, this application of the hooks is considered to be only one plausible version, which has been put forward by a very reputable scholar (*Ann Hyland. The Horse in the Ancient World, 2003*). However, this use has been recognized by modern science as the most realistic and likely[1].

No doubt, the object is an absolute rarity. It surfaced as the result of excavations of the temple of Artemis in the north of Greece. This sounds absolutely reasonable because the winners of sporting games or races sacrificed the bit of the winning horse to the temple in following with tradition.

Roman iron testifies to the Roman training traditions with absolute eloquence (see photo 1.20).

The Greek and Persian thorns disappeared, somewhat, in this form, but a certain trick was added that provided for breaking a shank at a right angle and, correspondingly, increasing the impact on the mouth. (It is understood that extremely few authentic Roman bits are left in the world, and I have preserved only a version which pertains to late Rome; theoretically these are Egyptian excavations from the times of Marc Antony). There likely were other examples, including those with spines. At least the poet Virgil advised riding horses using a curb bit with a high port and long shanks, with discs and thorns on the mouthpiece.

As shown by excavations of a Congaeti burial pit, in ancient Iberia, around the 4th century B.C., they also were not especially timid in the selection of painful methods of influencing the horse (see photo 1.21).

---

[1] Generally speaking, when a new type of equipment is discovered, quite a lot depends on the state of the rare object. A lot is determined by the researcher's ability to palpate the object, to fiddle with it and test it on a model. Ann Hyland probably did not even succeed in getting permission to photograph the bit for her original research and provided only its drawing in her book. It is not difficult to assume that no physical examination or tests have been carried out which is why the "mask" explanation should be approached with some prudence.

1.20. Roman
1st–3rd centuries

1.21. Transcaucasia
8th century B.C.

Complex bits related to multi-jointed snaffles with cheek pieces that have been excavated are typical for that era and also are designed to inflict acute and extraordinary pain in the region of the soft palate, as well as exert a constant strong painful impact on the gums and teeth. I would attribute them not to the Congaeti or Akhalgori cultures, but, rather, would classify them as typical equine accessories of Northern Parthia that ended up in the Congaeti burial mound as war trophies.

* * *

The Gothic era bequeathed to Europe a nasty riding seat in which the rider openly interfered with the horse's movement. This resulted in a tendency to terribly beat the horse, to use very bulky iron in the horse's mouth, and spurs with necks which reached as much 35 centimeters. But chiefly — the gothic seat contributed nothing to the

1.22. War curb bit with spikes
England, 15th century

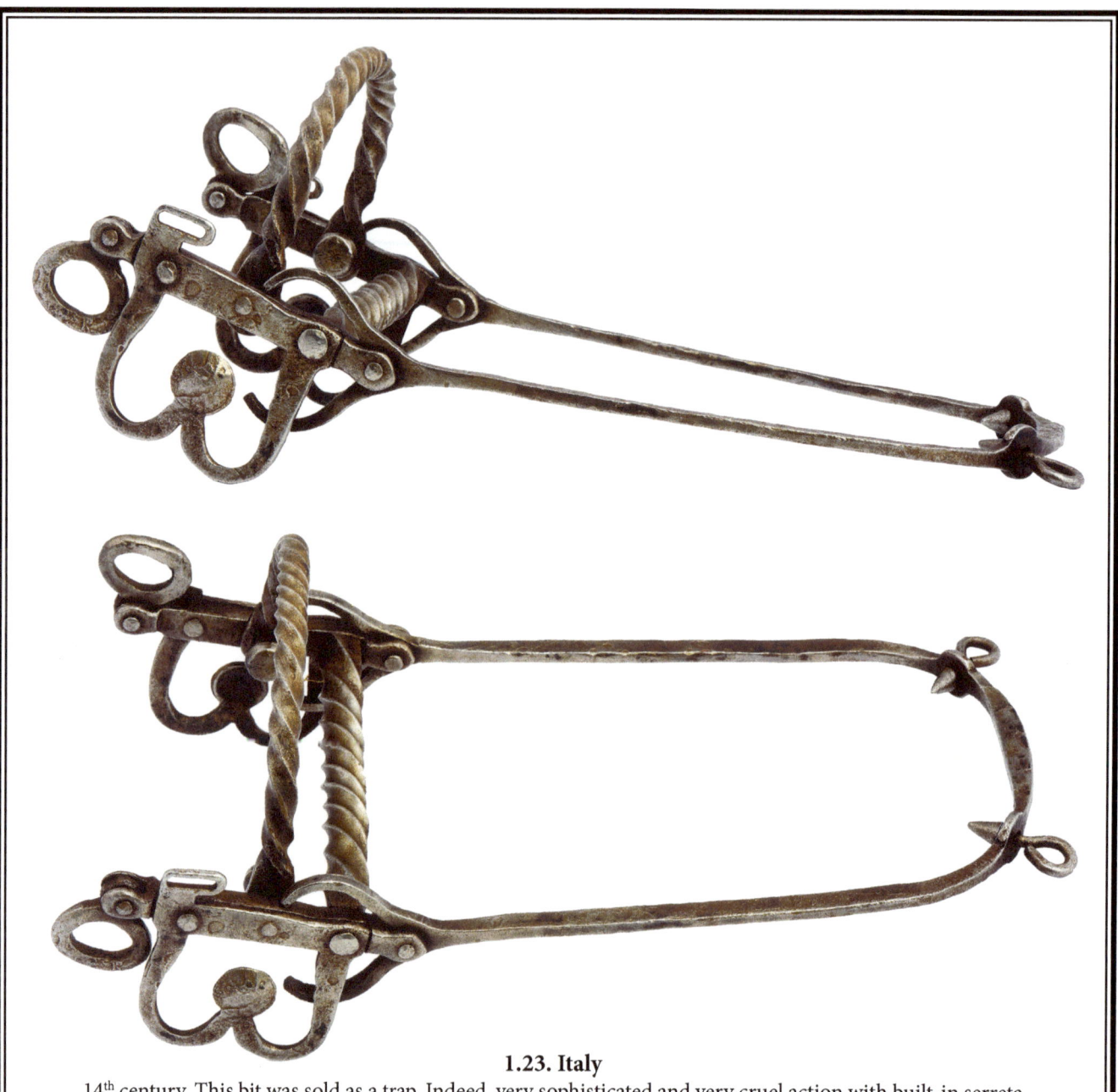

1.23. Italy
14th century. This bit was sold as a trap. Indeed, very sophisticated and very cruel action with built-in serreta.

1.24. Europe
15th–16th centuries

understanding of the horse's balance beneath the rider, even the horse could not find it.

Here, and further on in the text, I am examining only a certain upper class of horse in the equestrian world hierarchy created by man — namely, saddle horses.

Those horses, whom it would be possible to combine under the general category of "non-saddled" — draft horses, farm horses, carriage pullers, city dwellers — over the centuries had the same fate at the hands of all peoples. The fate and life of the workhorse of the Gothic era in no way differed from the fate and life of the ancient Egyptian horse or the horse of a Russian peasant. The fashion, trends, birth and death of the various schools in no way ever influenced the monstrous life of these horses, a life replete with beatings and other indignities.

The fundamental tasks of a saddle horse in Gothic times were the following:
- delivery of a load, in the form of a rider, roughly to where he needed to go;
- to trample and bite someone along the way wherever possible;
- not to die in a year's time from decaying and inflamed wounds and abrasions which were caused by armor and the very complex and always poorly fitting accoutrements.

The marching, fighting, tournament and parade horse of the middle ages simply carried the rider along a certain specified trajectory and it wasn't important what the trajectory was — from Paris to Liège or from the flag at one end of a tournament barrier to the flag at the other end.

The control of a horse was uncommonly crude and feeble.

Let's take the 14th and 15th century military curb bit that was standard for those times.

With a shank up to 50 centimeters long, the mouthpiece was provided with hooks for tearing up the palate and with spiked cylinders for the gums and to make a deep impact on the tongue (see photo 1.22).

And all for nothing… nothing except an extremely ordinary, tame ride at a trot and sometimes at a canter. It was all romanticized and poeticized, and later even motion pictures had a hand in promoting the fantasy.

The main practice was the so-called "ramming motion," a heavy, unbalanced trot which was the primary gait of any medieval attack.

* * *

The Arabian East, professing without exception the principle that "one must treat a horse in the barn as a friend and brother, but when you ride on it, as the most evil of enemies," also devised iron of an extreme nature.

Eyewitnesses described it as "terrible and agonizing horse equipment, which is so disastrous for horses that it can sometimes break their jaws and even crack their bones inside."

True, this "terrible and agonizing iron" of the 13th century would eventually be in common usage in Europe where it was called "Arabian," "Turkish," or simply "hunting" iron.

The eyewitnesses themselves described the style of Arabian riding.

Using their own, Arabian type of iron, these peoples rarely stopped a horse without filling its throat with blood or it being in a tormented, terrible and miserable condition.

"All of their horses are reined in powerfully by the sudden and powerful impulse of the Arabian curb bit, from which the whole croup sometimes is broken."

Despite the ferocity of these gadgets, the Arabian, and even any oriental rider, always was very primitive.

* * *

The Renaissance burst forth, which drove the first serious nail into the coffin of Gothic riding almost immediately, because it brought to god's earth classical ideals and the "picturesque ease," "elegance" and "power" of the "classical seat" — (that description being a myth if ever there was one).

The Renaissance, as you recall, rapidly became ingrained in life.
Translated into modern terms, it was an ordinary cultural revolution.
Gothic culture, including its style of riding, was destroyed in approximately 80 years.

* * *

France, the 17th century.
Here by this time the great riding school named Haute École, that is "high school," had been created, and had gained its fundamental features which maximized exploitation of the horse's capabilities.
And then we see the appearance of the Haute École masters, who finished off the old beliefs about riding and presented to the world examples of an unimaginable perfection and a fundamentally new way of riding, so-called "school riding."
And when it was understood that school riding is an art, magic and religion simultaneously, there was no end of those wishing to kiss the hems of the tunics of the gods of this religion, which is how the fathers of Haute École were presented to the public.
The blood princes, the grocers, the suppliers of lacy linens to the bordellos who had grown rich, the powdered provincial nobles, officers of all stripes, men of letters, kings, retired inquisitors, successful artisans, actors and grandees — they all rushed to learn and grasp school riding.

There are more than enough disgraceful and outrageous pages in the history of Haute École. But, in addition to cruelty and stupidity, there was also the determination to push ahead, all-in-all toward the light, to achieving the perfect balance of the horse, to her athletic development, and on the part of some of the "fathers," to maintaining the gentleness and trust of the horse.
For those days, it wasn't enough.
Haute École has at least eight canonized founding fathers.
They are Frederico Grisone, Giambattista Pignatelli, Salomon de la Broue, Cesare Fiaschi, Francois Robichon de la Guérinière, Chevalier de Nestier and Antoine de Pluvinel. These are the only legitimate, canonized fathers.
And I am not talking about any historical small potatoes that hint at their paternity in the memoirs of that time. There are about thirty men, and all of them, as they say, had their hands in it, but they were not canonized.
Both the canonized and minor fathers of Haute École were masters of very complex dressage. They were rough,

1.25. Turkey
17th century

    This is a very typical Ottoman curb. Made of steel, bronze, copper and coral, it weighs 945 grams; the shanks are 245 millimeters long. The mechanism of mouth impact is characteristic for the East. In Europe it is called "Arabian" or "Janett style" curb. Today it is widely used at races under the name "Chifney". The same principle is used in the leading out bridle design. From the curve of the mouthpiece a three-centimeter stem goes up and rests itself on the slope of the upper palate. The stem ends in a ring embracing the lower jaw and works at the slightest pull of the rein as a super chin chain. The peculiar part of its design is the location of high and sharp thorns on the straight elements of mouthpiece — three on each side. Their function was to prevent the horse from any attempts to insert a part of its tongue between the cheek branch and the ring stem. The curb is decorated with a typical pair of ornamented curves with polished corals "hung" on them. Seven corals have been lost but the device is so disgusting that, frankly speaking, taking any care of it seems hardly possible.

    History: According to the legend it was brought from the Russian-Turkish war as a trophy, then rested with a Moscow family before it got into the School collection. Only now, man-made collection using bits was taking the place of spurs of a hellish length — thus becoming a new variety of torture for the horse.

1.26. Europe, probably England
16th century

1.27. Praeceptor bit, France
16th–17th centuries

A relic of the School, a bit of the late 16th century, known as a praeceptor bit, is decorated with bronze "bossettes" on which we find the ancient emblem of the School — the staff of Moses entwined by the snake, topped with human and equine skulls and a triple key. However, it contains many secrets. Here's one of them. After making a series of complicated actions pressed on the rivets in a certain order the opening mechanism of the bossettes kicks in and it become clear that the real emblem, hidden behind the symbol of the School is the seal of the Knights Templar Order.

1.28. German curb
Beginning of the 16th century

This steel bit (weight —1460 g.; branch length — 290 mm; mouthpiece width — 137 mm.) is an absolute rarity. The origin is probably Germany as a very similar ornamentation of the branche segment of another curb bit is in the Armory collection in Wittenberg, where it's dated from the year 1649.

It should be remembered precisely that Germany has always been a country that is "outside" School influence, the country with the most barbaric culture of horsemanship (even considering that period of time). Furthermore, nothing was invented in Germany though

it made passable copies of all European innovations. This curb has never been redesigned or restored. A few of the elements that increase the severity of the mouthpiece, probably a hanging rosaire and coquille, have been lost. Of exceptional interest is the construction on the straight parts of the mouthpiece – cylindrical rotating drums, and, to enhance their effect, the outer rods of the drums are twisted. The boufettes are manufactured in the "pure" Gothic tradition, which is also a sign of its German roots, as the design and functions are late Renaissance while its décor is Gothic. This altogether is very typical for Germany with its aesthetic backwardness. The construction was copied from a European sample but the décor of the curb, as well as many other household appliances and tools, was carried out in accordance with the traditions of the remote lands of the German empire where Gothic trends in ornamentation and household décor survived long after the Gothic reign. The gourmette (curb chain) may seem incredible, rare or unbelievable but in fact its design is rather common and widespread among Gothic and School curbs. The gourmette has five links; three middle links make a solid chain. (This design was used later and is still used in the chains of bicycles and chainsaws.)

History: It was discovered in a private armory collection in the Baltic region having been transferred from the Kaliningrad region where it had been sharing glory and shelf space with a famous collection of keys and locks. I bought it inexpensively. As it is not considered arms, it didn't have any military value in the eyes of the collection owner.

1.29. Europe
14th–15th centuries

tough horsemen with dismal biographies and physiognomies, confirmed libertines, ready for a fight. Their commodity and their talent was in incredible demand.

While criticizing the savage methods of the founding fathers of the Haute École, one must always remember what exactly they had to break through after at least 25 centuries of absolute incomprehension of even primitive functions of a ridden horse.

They, of course, were great riders for their time. Great riders are born very, very rarely, more rarely than great violinists or great writers.

Now to the most unpleasant thing. All these "teachers," practically without exception, made use of extremely cruel, awful iron and without fail contributed to this problem something brand new — their very own, original designs.

To this very day, we classify rare bits according to the names of the Haute École maestros.

We say: "Here's the curb bit mouthpiece devised by the master Grisone, and this is what Pignatelli cannon looks like".

There are cannons invented by Fiaschi, Guérinière and Pluvinel.

The methods for training horses relied mainly on force and were often simply loathsome.

Grisone's regulation bit (see photo 1.33) was provided both with a sharp spade for piercing the upper palate, and additional chains for restraining the tongue, as well as long arms (31 cm). These arms, the so-called shanks or branches, were connected to each other for strength by two more chains that are called chainettes. I won't even talk about the crudeness and strength of the main curb chain, the gourmette, which put pressure on the trigeminus nerve and jaw bones from below.

Pignatelli's regulation iron is a bit more modest, without any special frills in the mouth, but just as murderously hard on the palate and the trigeminus nerve (see photo 1.41).

All Haute École curb bits, no matter what the design of the cannons, are based on the same principle and have an average shank length of 30–32 centimeters and a weight of approximately 550–600 grams. Owing to its length, the very powerful shank lever sets the curb bit mechanism into action with the slightest movement of the reins: the curb chain digs into the jaw bone, compressing the trigeminus nerve, and the port, a bend in the middle of the mouthpiece to form a raised arc, digs into the palate. The chainette holds the shanks tightly together; once slid apart, they would allow the bit to lie flat on the tongue; held together, the bit digs constantly into the horse's palate. Everything combined assures the maximum painful impact on the horse's mouth.

Jokers such as Grisone, Pignatelli and Fiaschi even invented special devices which were secured to the bit to maximize the painful impact.

They were the rosaire or the chapellette, steel beads which caused a sharply pressing action almost on the very root of the tongue; the trebuchet, which resembled a small catapult; or the coquille, shaped like a shell, which scraped the palate.

A rarer example of a device intended to increase the severity of the curb bit mouthpiece, the designer of which is not known, is called the chardon (all the elements of curb bit are presented in photo 1.30). It is a little mechanism which is set into action by the rider, who with a light pull of the rein exposes the special barbs so that they are brought into contact with the horse's mouth.

The "Chardon" curb (see photo 1.31) is an absolute rarity and convincing proof of the complexities of hippological history, reflecting the purposeful movement of "pre-School" equestrian Europe which pursued the de-

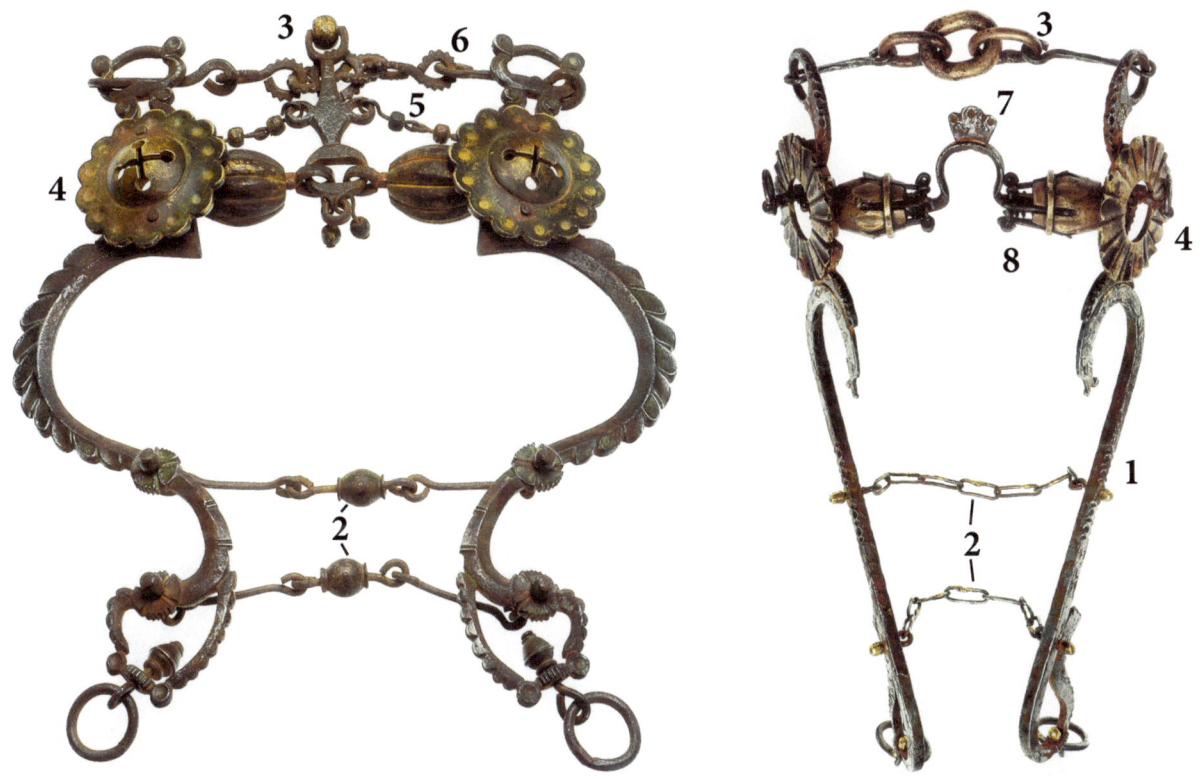

1.30. Parts of a curb bit
1 — branch; 2 — chainette; 3 — gourrmette; 4 — boufette; 5 — rosaire; 6 — trebuchet; 7 — coquille; 8 — chardon

velopment of pain inflicting properties of bits in order to achieve at least some control over the horse. I know only of two remaining curbs with chardon. I have one of them which can be seen in the above photo. Most likely it has nothing to do with the Haute École period, but it can be applied to the middle or even beginning of the 16th century. The second curb with chardon is kept in a closed private collection. I saw it. It's newer and has to do with the beginning of the 17th century. It's amazing but the mechanisms of the thorn ejection still work.

My "Chardon" curb is manufactured with all possible skill and care.

Bronze. Steel. Copper. Gold Leaf. Weight — 1357 g. Length of branches — 37.5 cm (right), 37.2 cm (left). Width of mouth piece — 13.8 cm. The mechanism which controls the emerging thorns is located on both halves of the mouthpiece which is joined with the help of a steel arch in the shape of a horseshoe with a typical early coquille. This mechanism has survived up to the present day and it is carefully adjusted.

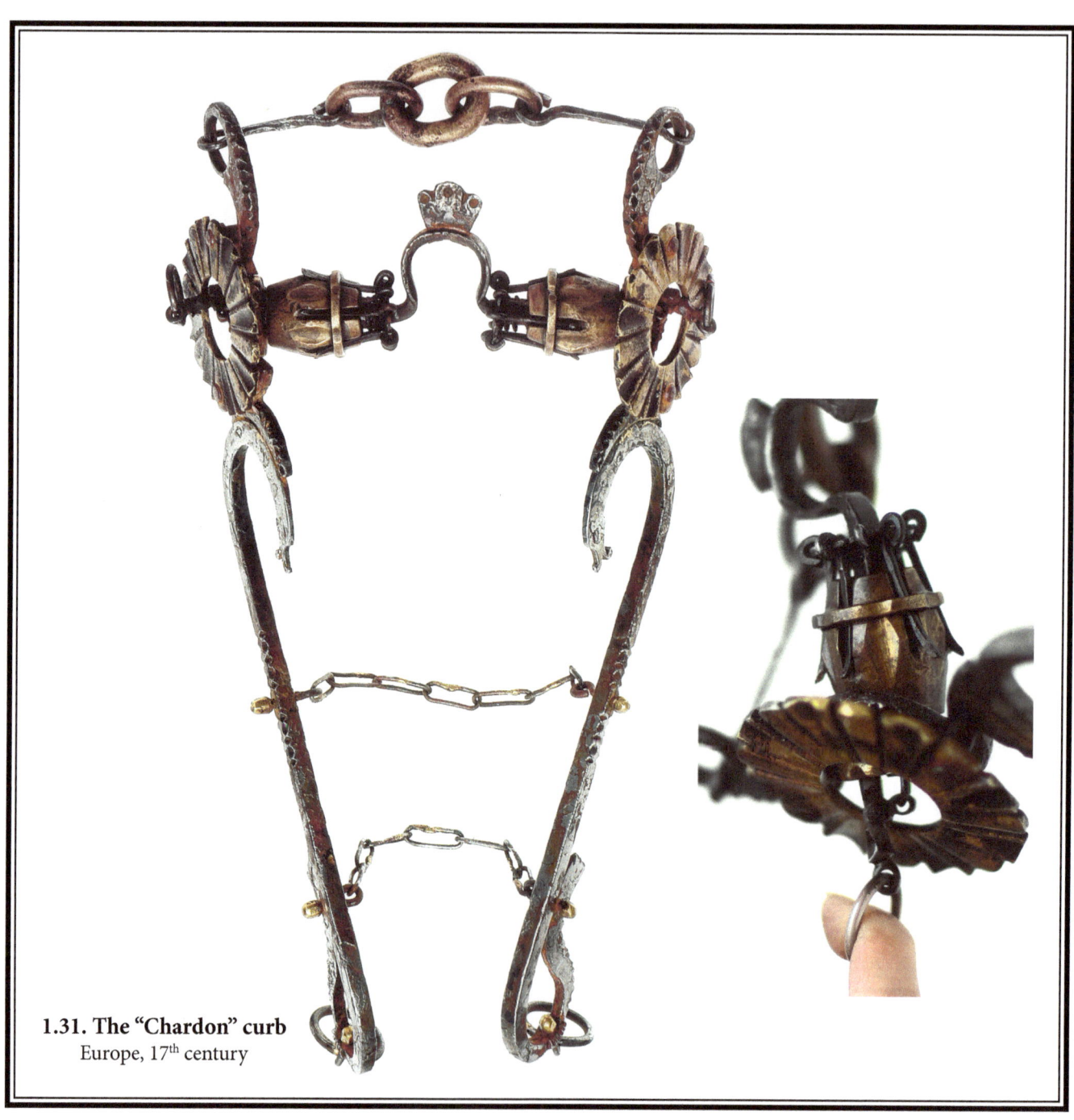

1.31. The "Chardon" curb
Europe, 17th century

With a finger lightly pulling the ring which sticks out from a boufette, the thorns emerge. Whenever you stop they retreat back into their part of the mouthpiece, into special grooves.

Apart from the main bridle-rein which was fastened to the rings below the double chainette, there was an additional rein attached to the ring which opens the thorny flower mechanism.

I can't identify with confidence the country of origin of the curb as mechanical appliances were equally fashionable everywhere from Holland to England.

The curb looks well preserved but it is sure to have gone through substantial cleaning. Numerous cavities of different depths in the steel of the branches prove that the metal had been in a cocoon of rust but has been cleaned. Moreover no acids were used for the purpose so it took much time and effort to carry out this manual work.

The rust in some parts has destroyed the metal by making it thinner in some places, and in some parts has left cavities of varying depths. It was discovered that the curb has never been taken apart for cleaning. The juncture of the mouthpiece and branch is knitted together and has never been exposed. The rivets which fasten the boufette are typical for the 16th century. It is peculiar that in spite of some looseness they are identical.

Their being loose doesn't mean frequent use of the curb but since rust damaged the rivets they grew thinner and finally loosened up. Branch segments are soldered with silver. Both chainettes are genuine. But the original gourmette has been lost, so in trying to recreate the historic wholeness of the curb I detached a gourmette from another 16th century curb and attached it for the photo session (this kind of curb chain was in wide use in the 16th century).

Thorough cleaning of the curb deprived me of the opportunity to carry out a number of biological tests and find out how many horses left their blood and saliva in the nooks of the mechanism. Cleaning wiped them out from all the available surfaces. Obviously some remains can be found somewhere in the depths under the springs and rivets but to make these probes one needs to dismantle the curb which could be disastrous for the fragile and rust-eaten mechanism.

The damaging power of the mechanism is beyond any doubt.

It's clear that after being applied for a few seconds it could kill any horse by completely depriving her of an ability to eat.

But even without the chardon and the trebuchet, the iron of that era is monstrous in its force of impact.

* * *

We can safely say that the precise scientific and practical knowledge of the torturous role of any equine iron (i. e. bits) celebrates its 400th birthday now. In the beginning of the 17th century in France Haute École master Salomon de la Brue published the result of his research which he called "PRECEPTES".

There is a complete analysis of the effect the bit causes in a horse's mouth.

It is noteworthy that la Brue had studied the principles of the effect of the bit not to comminate the horse torturers or even to express his dismay. He did it only to make his own inventions more effective.

1.32. Europe
16th century

1.33. France
16th century

1.34. School curb, France
The beginning of 17th century

    This School curb is made of steel, bronze, gold, iron, copper and silver. It weighs 1100 grams with 30 centimeter long branches and a mouthpiece width of 14 centimeters. Even without restoration it maintains excellent integrity.
    The branches, now dirtied gilt, are made as laughing dolphins, yet the boufette and the providing structure is missing. The mouth piece is a complex type called Padane. It has two free-wheeling spheres with raised notches on the circumference and a cogged wheel in the center. Dimples were hammered into the inside of the mouthpiece during the original forging. Rozières from the branches to the mouthpiece bend have seven copper rings each. Construction includes interlocking flattened bronze wire, steel hooks of hard-tempered steel and loose joints.
    There is silver soldering, but no gilding on the mouthpiece. However on the lateral freewheeling spheres there are irregular impressions left from first and second premolars that imply use by many horses of different mouth size.
    There are thinned areas on the rein rings, as well as distortion that prove this curb bit was used often for a long period of time.
    The bossette (the lower chains between branches) probably reflects the beginning of 19th century. They are roughly mounted with another kind of flattening, tin soldering and a different type of copper.

1.35. Europe
16th century

1.36. Europe
16th century

1.37. Europe
17th century

1.38. Europe
Late 16th century

1.39. Europe
17th century

1.40. Europe
17th century

1.41. Europe
17th century

1.42. Europe
17th century

The thing is, that la Brue was not only the very reputable School dressage master, but also the most famous constructor, mechanic and designer of bits.

He wanted to make his creations absolute in their painful impact, but also to make them the way that a horse would not die immediately after those creations were used upon him. A horse also was not to sustain serious injuries of the mouth.

La Brue dissected dead horses at the slaughterhouses; he had prosected their mouths while cutting off their tongues, gums and palatal vaults. He was the first to "dig" into the horse's mouth and to make the bit construction an exact science.

La Brue invented about thirty types of curb bits. He described another 28 types of them, improved them and left the detailed and systematized description to his students and descendants in his treatise "The Canon of Monseigneur la Brue".

Here you can see the curb bit of the "Padane" type (see photo 1.34). We can not be sure that this specific bit was made by la Brue himself, but it is known that this type was not the fashion for very long. No more than twenty years. All the known specimens were made in the la Brue workshop (or they were rumored to be made there). This type came to disuse because of the severe injuries it inflicted upon horses and under the constraint of some School Masters. Although, the principle of the "Padane" is not the real invention of Brue. It is likely that he had taken the idea of the "Arabian" curb bit which has a slightly different construction but the same principle. The well-known racing Chifney bit which is still used nowadays has inherited the principle of the "Padane".

* * *

The end of the 18th century did not bring anything new to the art of riding; actually, it would become considerably more primitive and crude.

The artificial balancing of a horse through iron in her mouth and the displaced croup discovered by the founding fathers of Haute École would become the standard everywhere except the cavalry.

But! Complex elements which required a rider's virtuosity were virtually disappearing.

The fact of the matter is that in France, the French revolutionaries who had put the great manèges out of business and shot the students and masters, so enthusiastically finished off Haute École, which was seen as a completely aristocratic attribute, with the butts of their rifles.

(The revolutionaries used de la Guérinière's famous manège for meetings of their schizoid tribunals.)

True, it wasn't only in the revolution.

By the middle of the 18th century, two deadly enemies to Haute École tradition had appeared.

The "High School's" first enemy was the cavalry, with its desire to see the horse only as fodder for one or two battles and as a means of transport.

The second enemy was the Anglomania which infected Haute École's homeland with a love for things primitive and the excitement of races.

Two non-canonized masters of the School deserve special respect and a posthumous good word: D'Abzac and de la Bigne. These two struggled desperately, both in the manèges and in living rooms, with the English influence that was so disastrous for the School. England, with its races, with a veneration for abominable riding and with its primitivism and coarseness with regard to

1.43. School curb, France
The beginning of the 18th century

man and horse, turned out to be the grave digger of the art of riding.

D'Abzac forbade everything English in the manège, including the English style of boots and the English hunting whips that were coming into fashion then.

De la Bigne refused to take even the most profitable and titled pupils only because they were English. These two, unfortunately, were in the minority.

"English style," the style of red-nosed squires who recklessly rode after the fox, was killing school riding with its search for contact with the horse, its complexity and inspiration.

England was victorious because she was able to offer the world more primitive, democratic riding standards which by the 19th century had already completely forced out Haute École.

Conflict between the pro-cavalry academies and the classical schools began to appear as early as the 18th century.

The Saumur school, founded in 1763, was the main ideologue of military horsemanship, having united the Luneville, Angers and Saint Germain schools under a banner of hostility to the "academicians."

Resisting them was only the Versailles school which had maintained authentic classical traditions, that is, those

1.44. Europe
Late 18th century

which professed a fine, masterly and sparing practice for the horse in comparison with the primitive cavalry.

It didn't resist for long, and then its foundations, too, were shaken by the influence of the cavalry generals and society's enthusiasm for English races; soon Versailles traditions were totally, physically, eradicated.

Into the basket beneath the guillotine of the French revolution, along with pomaded and empty heads slid, in the best traditions of the gallant age, unfortunately, also the severed head of Haute École.

The art of riding, per se, was returning to the level of the 15th century.

"Clowns" like F. Baucher, the Golden Duke or J. Fillis spent hours collecting a horse and taught this to their adherents.

The severity of the iron — the curb bit — of this time was the last straw. Take for example this generally rustic curb bit of the "Jineta" type, weighing 850 grams, with a boffette of carved bronze and a shank 20 centimeters long. Here it is easy to notice that the four-link curb chain, which is traditional for Haute École curb bits, has been replaced by a steel pear-shaped ring, which clasps the horse's lower jaw, not so much to be able to affect the trigeminus nerve, as simply to break the jaw with a light pull of the rein (see photo 1.43).

This type of iron was so widespread that it even has been cited in a number of typical works, in *L'Encyclopedie* by Diderot and d'Alembert in the volume *Art du Cheval*, in the chapter "Eperonier". This mouthpiece of a curb bit is, per se, the European version of the common Arabian iron discussed above.

1.45. England
Late 18th century

Made of steel, bronze, copper and silver this curb weighs in at 1630 g. The shanks are 290 mm. and the mouthpiece measures 130 mm.

This is a typical carriage curb of the middle of the 18th century. At the beginning of the 20th century it underwent a rough restoration — the bases of the boufette were replaced. The round silver badges were replaced by copper ones coarsely riveted.

These copper badges are rather poorly patterned but the original crowns from the previous boufette have been transferred onto them. I claim that with confidence because this type of curb is a common attribute of six horse carriages and there are lots of them which have survived until today. As a rule the material of boufette is identical to the material of their additional patterned covers. The mouthpiece is crudely manufactured and of the most coarse type, practically triangle in shape. It has long been in use and has broken so many horse's teeth and perforated so many palates. On the mouthpiece there are innumerable teeth marks from different horses.

History: I bought this curb at a store belonging to a fat Hindu. It was kept in a huge old cap under a pile of hardened leather bridles for a six horse harness decorated with the same plated silver patterns as found on the shanks of the bit.

1.46. Europe
18th century. Bronze gilt

1.47. Radjasthan bit
Late 19th–20th centuries

1.48. England
18th century

The 18th century itself returned to the ancient tradition of installing sprocket teeth on the bit, which, ramming the palate vault, sharply impacted the minor palatine nerve and the maxillary nerve branch (see photo 1.44). Moreover, the mouthpiece designs were solid again, they were no longer jointed. Because of the solid-mouthpiece design, the severity of equine iron was growing extensively, and its destructive force was growing as well (see photos 1.45, 1.46, 1.48). From the 20th century into the 21st century, the snaffle bit has not changed at all.

* * *

Modern equestrianism has put two types of iron— the trigeminal and the dental — in the horse's mouth at the same time.

The curb bit with a mouthpiece resembling Pignatelli iron, except that it is even more severe, is shoved into the horse's mouth. Moreover, the mouthpieces are in no way designed differently than the Mongolian or Scythian ones. As we might expect, nothing startling happens.

Moreover, competitive or sporting dressage, timidly hinting that it is one of the "High School's" heirs, proves to be completely unable to reproduce the really complex and spectacular elements like the terre à terre, the capriole or the sentavo.

1.49. Curb bit of WWI
Germany

Only the most primitive elements, such as the passage and pirouette remain. And this is despite the fact that the horse's undisguised agony, which continues for hours — a combination of the effects of the different irons, the blows, the forced collection, mutilation of the neck and spine, the use of electrical shock and striking of the legs — has become the absolute norm. In this respect Haute École's fathers must be given their due, for they did not commit the sin of striking the legs, that is, rhythmic beating with sticks on the horse's legs in order to attain a higher lift of the legs in the passage, the piaffe and the balancer.

However, today's dressage "queens," be they Russian, German, or from anywhere else in the world, generally do not operate without striking the horse's legs.

Moreover, while in the classical schools (the Royal Andalusian, the Spanish School in Vienna) patterned in the image of the Haute École, exercises with the horse continue not more than half an hour, sporting dressage torments the horse for hours on end, with sessions lasting two or three hours each.

And still the result is nil.

This means that the severity of the iron gives no help toward revealing the horse's startling capabilities.

That same monolithic mouthpiece of the curb bit is still crammed into the arch of the horse's palate, we still fasten that same chain that causes painful paralysis with its strong pressure on the trigeminus nerve.

And it is used in precisely the same way.

1.50. Spade bit
Origin and age unknown, probably California, 19th century

Besides the unbelievable severity of the bit itself, its cruelty is assured by the extra iron tooth at the end of the port.

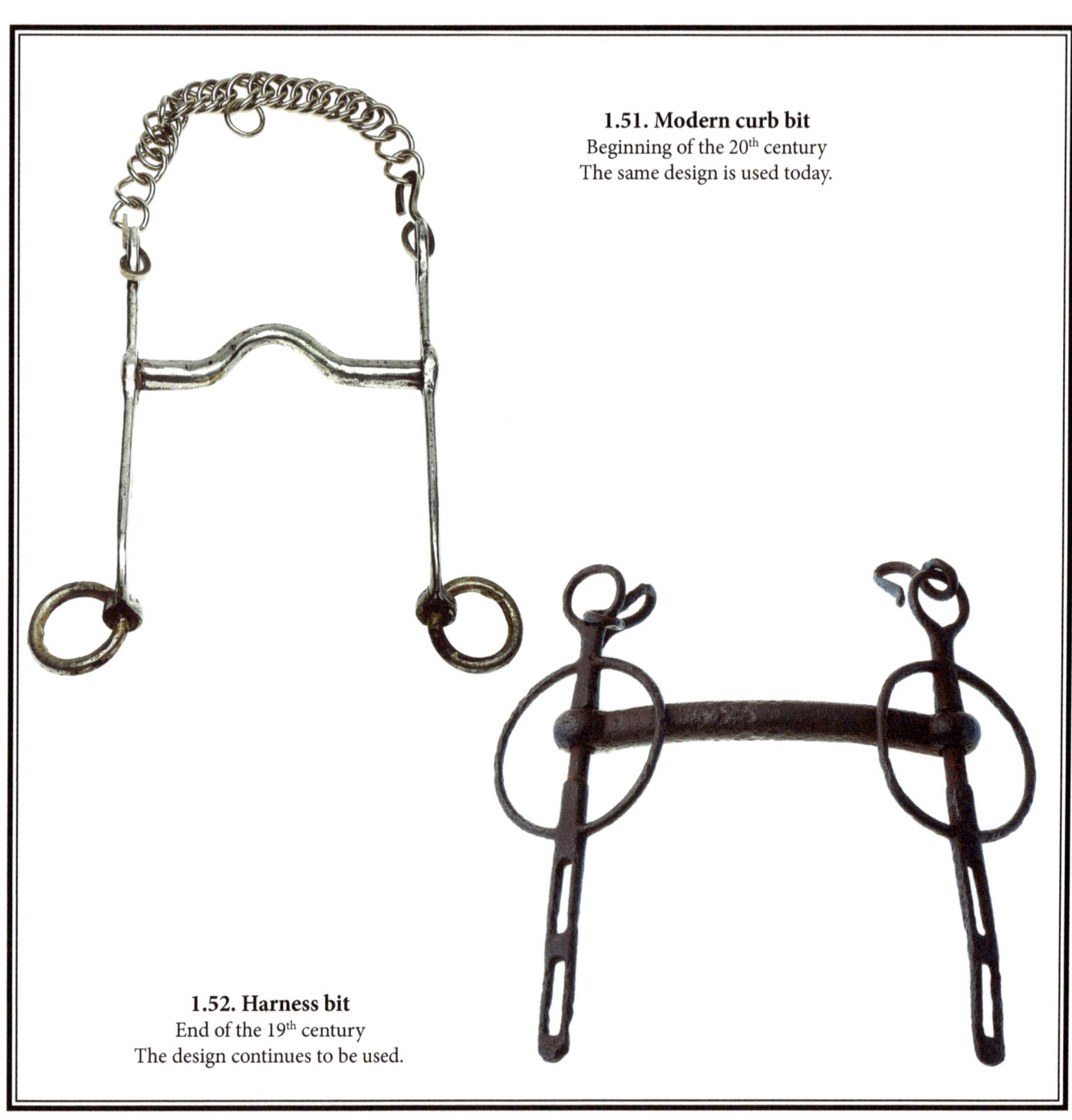

1.51. Modern curb bit
Beginning of the 20th century
The same design is used today.

1.52. Harness bit
End of the 19th century
The design continues to be used.

1.53. Kimblewick bit
20th century

The curb has become a bit less intricate, the shanks have been shortened somewhat, different metals have appeared, but its essence has not changed at all.

Only the design is different. The rosaire, chappellete, trebuchet and coquille have disappeared, because it has become clear that for the purpose of inflicting very strong pain and to have an effect on the main nerves of the head, a fixed bit, either with a curved port mouthpiece or a mouthpiece which is broken in two, is fully sufficient.

The colossal shank length disappeared on its own, because any ignoramus was able to break the jaw of too many horses too easily, which meant that the horse simply was murdered, since it became unable to eat and slowly, before everyone's eyes, died of starvation.

Plainly speaking, the rate of attrition was too high.

A principle was at work which generally governs the modern physical culture of primates, the "law of economy."

For efficient torture of the horse, the shank length of modern curb bits is all that is necessary.

* * *

The invention and usage of a sharp-toothed **serreta** (the creator is unknown, but possibly that very same Fiaschi) added a constant pain on the horse's muzzle to the pain caused by the iron.

This Serreta-type noseband (see photos 1.54, 1.55) was widely used by the European riding schools over a long period. The example shown is intended to be used exclusively with the curb while riding on horseback. The serreta-type

IRON

1.54. Serreta (Cavesson)
Europe, 16th century

1.55. Serreta (Cavesson)
Austria, 18th century

noseband has a pressing and crushing effect on the horse's soft tissue and nasal bone with every slight movement of the reins. Later, when brought to Latin America by the Spanish conquerors, it was modified into a bosal. When people specializing in ancient weapons and armory happen to come upon these relics in their collections they seldom, if ever, take the trouble of identifying their function and origin.

This serreta-type noseband (photo 1.54) was described as "an old spur of an odd design" when purchased! It is 247 grams of twisted steel, of which the inner section of the twist is inlaid with short sharp serrations.

This example (see photo 1.55) functions in the way that is typical of all the serreta-type nosebands and all the nasal appliances in general. It dates back as far as the late Medieval Ages, Renaissance and Baroque periods. Weight – 430 grams. Brass with traces of gilt.

Its Austrian origin is evident as it comes in a set, with spurs of the same design covered with the same gilt and having the same Vienna trademark. This Serreta-type noseband is likely to belong to the Vienna School (The Spanish Riding School) as its name implies.

This riding tool is still a compulsory component of Spanish riding. Today classical riding-school gurus have come to some disagreement about the terminology. All of them without exception use this nasal instrument but refer to it by different names. Luraschi prefers the word "Mediacane", the Royal Andalusian School of Equestrian Art call it a "Cavesson" and in 18th century Russian hippological treatises it was labeled as "Captsun" (*"капцунъ"*).

1.56. Poland
18th century, the original mouthpiece was replaced with a jointed piece in the 20th century

1.57. France
Early 19th century, the original mouthpiece has been substituted by a modern, "mild" snaffle

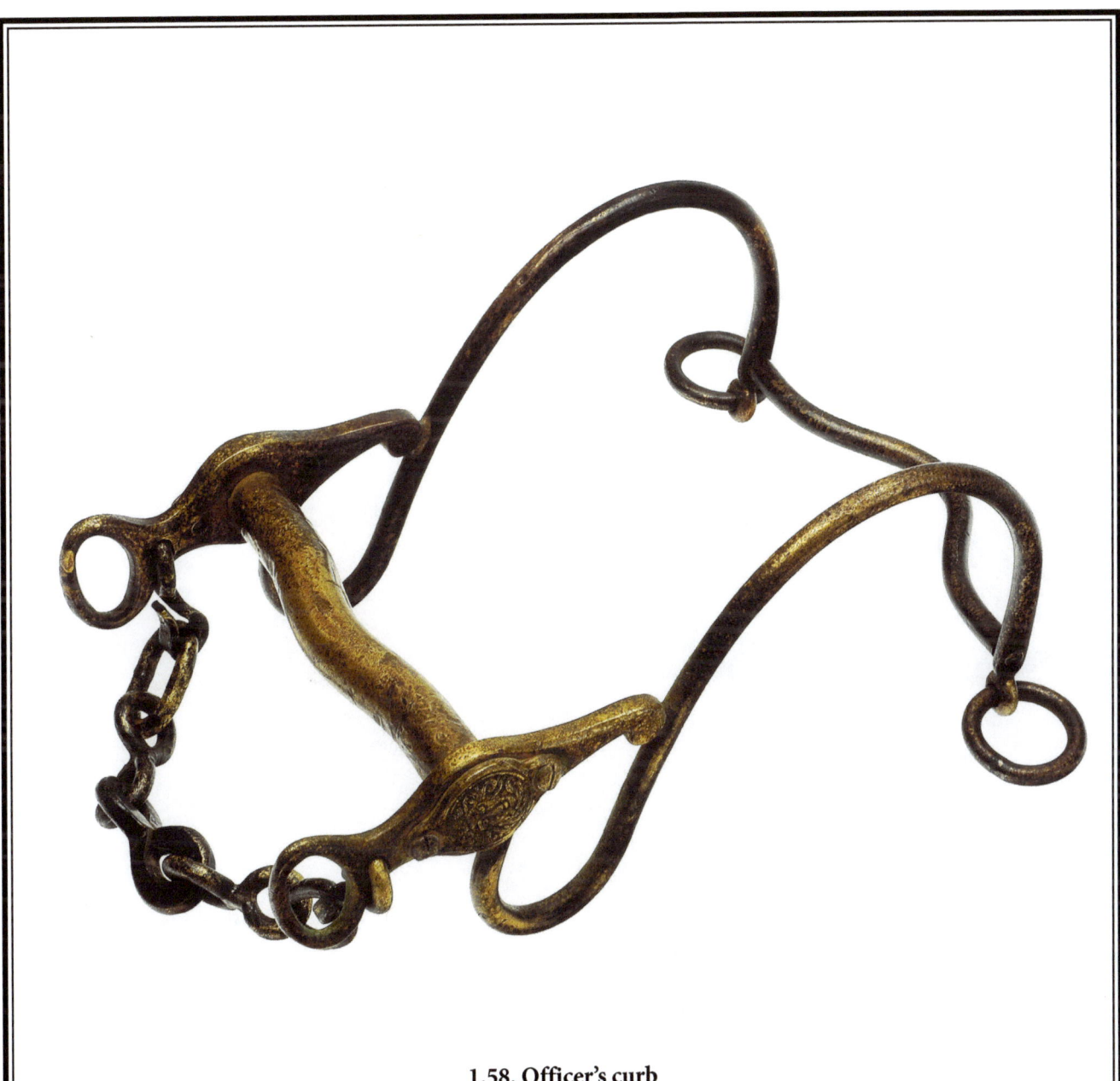

1.58. Officer's curb
France, middle 19th century

1.59. England
End of 19th century, bronze, ivory, silver

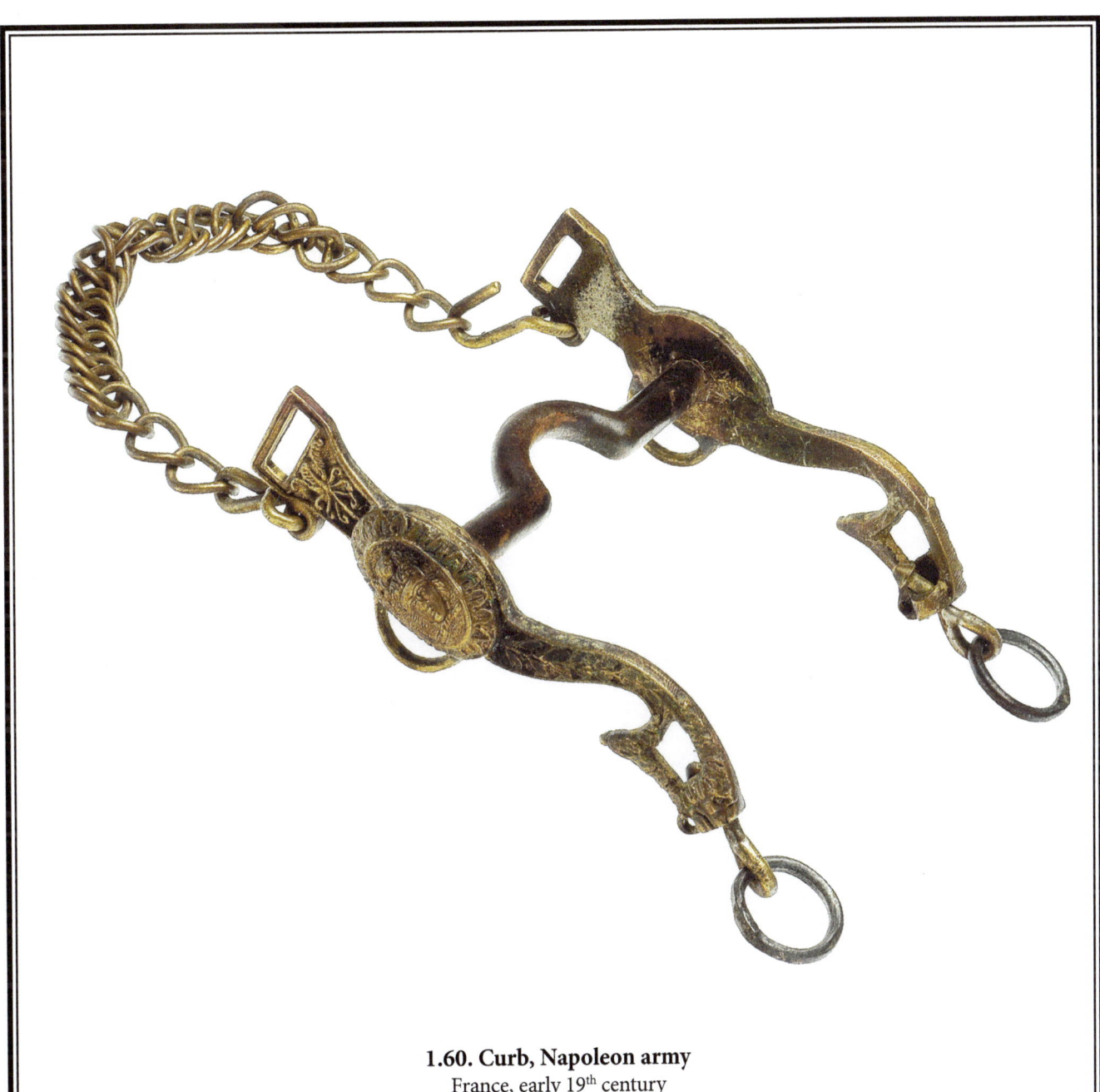

1.60. Curb, Napoleon army
France, early 19th century

1.61. Officer's Curb, France, Second Empire
19th century

CHAPTER 2
STIRRUPS

2.1. Unknown origin, probably Turkey
Unidentified age

Classification of stirrups is not a difficult issue. Some of them can be classified according to famous work of La Valetta. Others can be classified with the help of collections from Saumur castle, Mario Luraschi, The Hermitage in Saint-Petersburg and private museum collections in Europe. Fortunately I managed to know and study these collections. As for stirrups their origin and use are dated from the 4th up to 12th centuries. We have used absolutely authoritative sources which allow us to identify and date any ancient stirrups to a specific century based upon their form and materials. These descriptions and precise sketches of stirrups are from excavations of V. Mazhitov, Mriasimovsky, Murkaevsky, Ishimbaevsky, Lagerevsky, First Husainovsky, Yamashi-Taussky and other burrows of the South Ural. There are descriptions of objects found in cremation burials of northwestern Altai.

There are fundamental works called "USSR Archaeology" where all excavated finds are fully described and sketched. These are related to nomadic antiquities of Eastern Europe and Middle Asia during the 5th–8th centuries, Siberian antiquities, and finds in burrows of the East European prairie. With the help of this literature we can quite precisely classify and define according to origin any equine iron: stirrups, bits, cheek pieces or saddle girth buckles or bridle decoration. Identifying iron for private and state collections I always use these precious books and I haven't made a mistake yet. However, in the following tables with descriptions of stirrups, spurs, curbs, serretas I mention only models I know and have studied thoroughly, dated and classified. I want to thank the most distinguished Russian collector of our days, keeper of millions of Russian antiquities, a great specialist and my friend, Mikhail Surov, who groaning and grieving but without any word of objection suffered my predatory raids to the reserves of his huge collection. I was taking, I am taking and I will be taking everything that has the slightest connection with equine accoutrement.

* * *

Stirrups are considered the greatest invention, although their significance for arranging the correct seat is quite overstated.

Who invented stirrups is the greatest of mysteries, the answer to which will be clear in about 150 years, when all the possible archaeological discoveries which still have not happened will be made, all the results of the diggings for the last 200 years compiled and the undisputed timeline of the exhibit exposed in a strictly scientific and archaeological way. Consequently, the credit for invention of the stirrup will go to one or the other persons.

At the present time, I know of approximately 18 existing versions of the invention of stirrups in which the inventors are variously said to be the Celts, Chinese, Huns, Sarmats and Alans, the ancient Hindus, Romans, the Syanbi, and even Altai Turkic peoples.

But who invented them isn't all that important.

The reason for their invention is much more interesting.

Military historians, who in the best case may have sat on a rented horse once in their lives (whereby they immediately lost their pince-nez and berets and afterwards went around in the kind of haze that happens after an event like giving birth to twins), zealously allude and agree to the impossibility of the ancient riders being able to shoot, hack and stab without anything on which to rest their feet.

Supposedly these specific necessities of fighting provoked the invention of stirrups.

What a lot of rubbish!

Some fool dreamed this up a long time ago, and the rest repeat it like parrots.

It is certainly possible to fire a bow without depending on stirrups.

"Hacking" and "stabbing" without stirrups also pose no problems as long as there is a very high degree of true control of the horse (to the millimeter). This has been proven by me, as well as by very many stunt people who go to war on horses in the movies without saddles and stirrups.

I shall explain.

The success of the blow, whether chopping or stabbing, depends only on how precisely the horse is controlled, whether he is able to pass an enemy at a gallop at a "hand and blade" distance. (I am simplifying it somewhat in order not to beat around the bush.)

Simply put, if the horse were to get too close to the enemy, maintaining a distance of just half a blade length, or about 50 centimeters, the blow will not work out.

If it has taken an extra 50 centimeters the other way, the blow also will not work out.

If the horse were to be too frisky and break out of the requisite correct, measured gallop, it would be impossible to strike the blow. Similarly, if the horse were a bit too slow there also would be no result.

So, the secret of delivering a good, effective blow lies not in whether or not there are stirrups, but in the control of the horse.

Generally, stirrups have nothing to do with that.

And they weren't invented for easing the soldier's labor, either.

Stirrups were unable to ease anything, because a jaded horse cannot be controlled. By jaded I mean a horse not in collection, one for whom positioning his hind legs beneath his body and releasing the poll have not become a habit and standard for movement.

Furthermore, the Huns, Turks, Celts, Hindus and the Syanbi were all separated from the main Haute École invention by at least eleven centuries. So it's not a matter of stirrups, and there was no "stirrup revolution," about which today's historians, who have no notion of what a horse is or how to control him, love to write.

Curiously enough, it's a different reason.

And it's not even that it wasn't very convenient to climb onto a horse.

Hippocratic evidence has been preserved that the Scythians and other peoples who were accustomed to riding for a long time suffered from the worst edema, tumors, and inflammation of the legs because their legs were in a hanging position for a very long time, and the blood supply infracted the feet.

Not having colluded with Hippocrates, the Roman physician Galen describes approximately the same symptoms in Roman soldiers.

The doctors were not wrong this time.

Being still young and very stupid, I decided to test Hippocrates and Galen's assertion for myself. I ascertained, that in reality, it took not five or six hours, but only three hours of riding without a saddle with my legs hanging free like spaghetti before my legs were swelling and growing numb.

This was, probably, the main reason that prompted riding man to invent some kind of support for the feet.

2.2. Stirrups:
1 — the Don River, right side, 8th century; 2 — Iran, 17th century; 3 — India and Africa, 19th century; 4 — Slavic, 8th century

2.3. Stirrups:
1 — Caucasian, 19th century; 2 — Franks, 7th century; 3 — Pechenegs, 8th century; 4 — Normans, 10th century

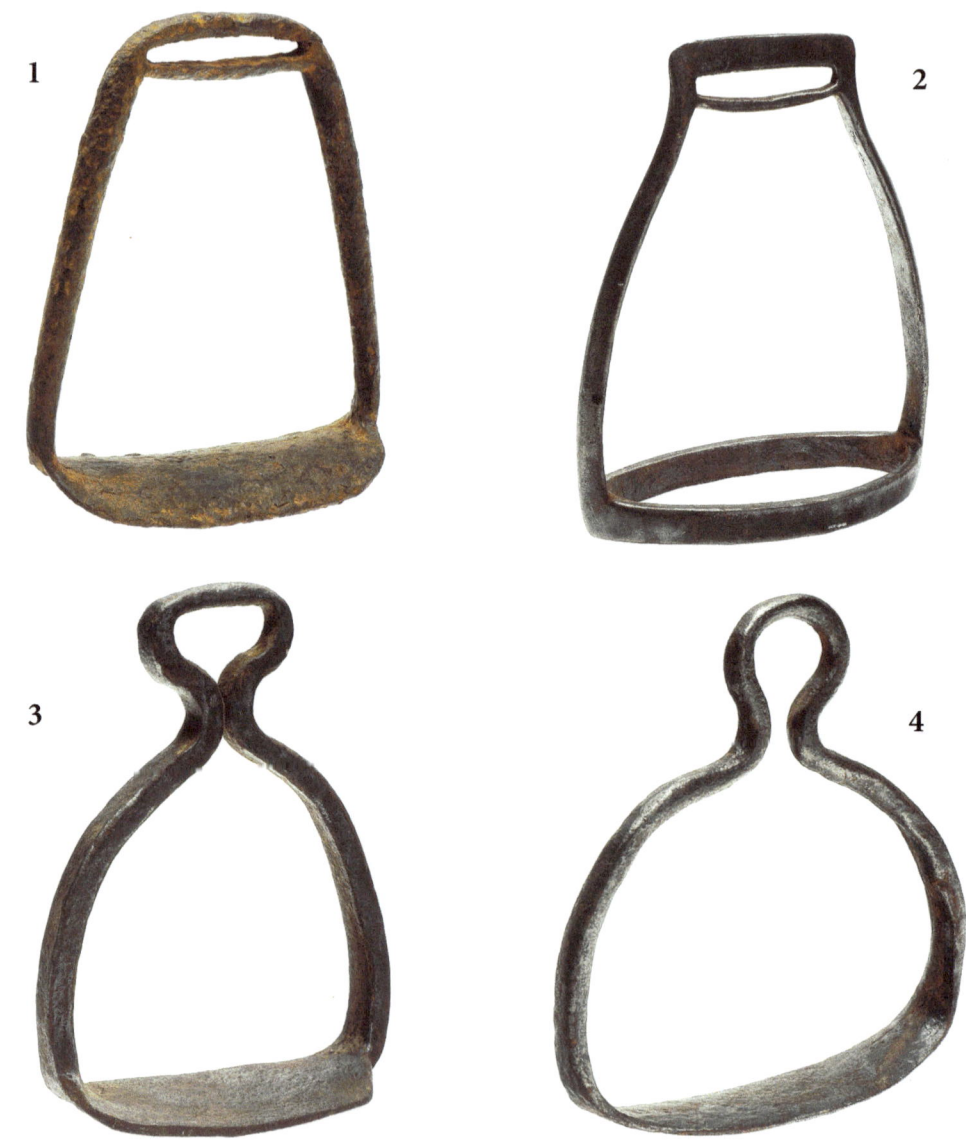

2.4. Stirrups:
1 — Mongolia, 11th–13th centuries; 2 — Russian cavalry, 19th century; 3 — Saxony, 10th century; 4 — India, 19th century

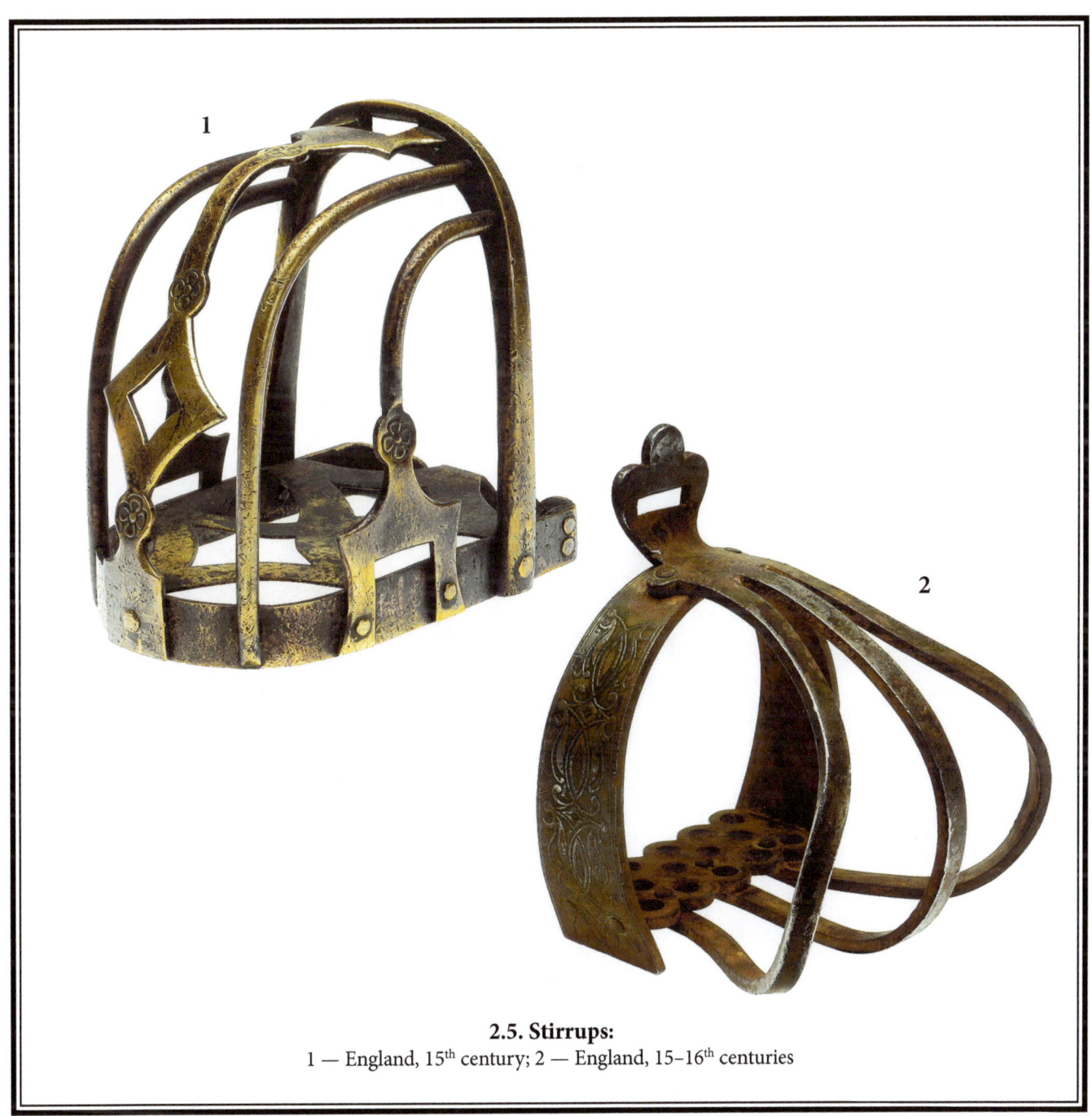

2.5. Stirrups:
1 — England, 15th century; 2 — England, 15–16th centuries

2.6 Europe
16th century

2.7 Gothic
End of the 14th — beginning of the 15th centuries

2.8. Stirrups:
1 — Europe, unknown age; 2 — Italy, 15th century

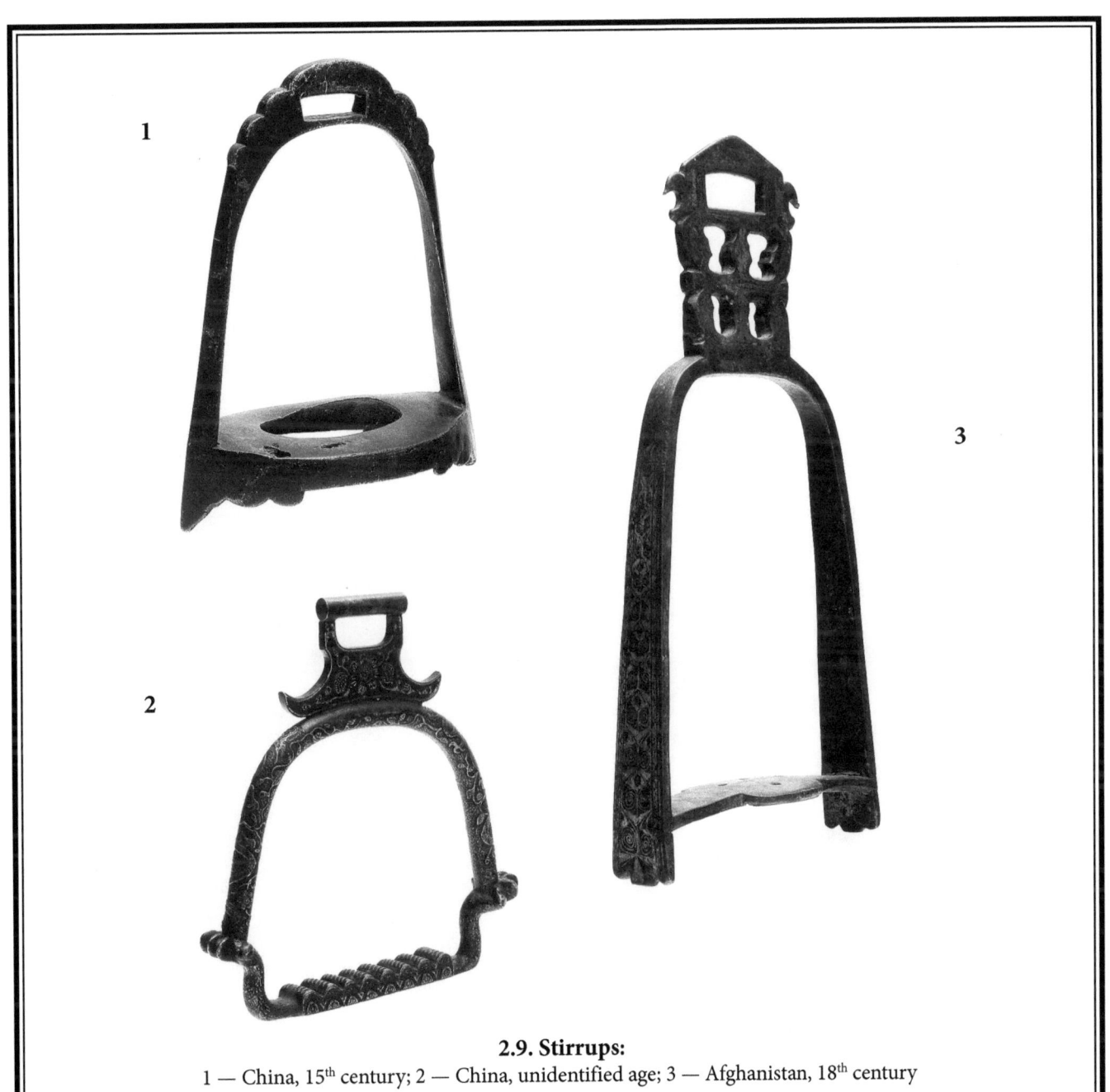

2.9. Stirrups:
1 — China, 15th century; 2 — China, unidentified age; 3 — Afghanistan, 18th century

2.10. Stirrups:
1 — Unknown origin, 19th century; 2 — Europe, 19th century; 3 — Flanders, 18th century; 4 — Lithuania, 17th century

2.11. Stirrups:
1 — Europe, 18th century; 2 — France, 18th century; 3 — France, 17th century; 4 — Austria, 18th century

2.12 France
17th century, Pluvinel School

2.13. Stirrups:
1 — France, 18th century; 2 — France, 17th century; 3 — France, 19th century; 4 — Saxony, 18th century

2.14. Stirrups:
1 — Russia, 19th century; 2 — South America, 19th century; 3 — Stirrup from woman's side saddle, South America, 18th–19th centuries; 4 — Spain, 17th–20th centuries (in use till modern times)

2.15. Stirrups:
1 a–b — Russia, 19th century; 2 — France, 19th century; 3 — Germany, early 20th century

2.16. Stirrup
Italy (?). The 14th century (?)

Cast and carved bronze — 626 g. Original soldering with silver, repair with tin. Width — 157 mm. Depth of footing — 65 mm.

Its Italian origin is rather disputable, as "fishes" in the upper part of the stirrup are typical for the German items. But this kind of stirrup is traditionally labeled as "Italian".

Nevertheless this type of stirrup has never been considered a typical one. These similar stirrups were manufactured as elements of a set of riding equipment. Dating and national identity are the same.

The stirrup's history is unclear; they were bought at the famous flea market Portobello in London. There is a solitary gloomy looking retail shop full of boxes with rotten, stone-like leather, rotten saddlecloths, ancient bridles, and 5-kilo-piles of the old guard spurs and buckles of all ages. If you search in the box purposefully you are likely to find carriage bits of the 18th century, ancient heel spurs, army temporal badges dating back to the Boer campaign... as well as the rarities like these "Italian Gothic stirrups".

It is hardly possible to find out if the contents of these boxes are some old stable inventory or possessions of a collector dedicated to an equine theme. At the beginning of the century this shop was acquired by a fat Hindu trading in eye-catching embroideries and packages of cinnamon and lighters. He prefers not to dwell upon the boxes and their contents inherited from the previous shop-owner. Being permanently obsessed with loud disputes with the same stout looking merchant from Pakistan who sells second hand umbrellas in the neighboring store he completely ignores any questions.

I have been dropping into his shop twice a year for five years to witness their everlasting dialogue.

The Hindu man got used to me and when I excavate some relic and show him the salesman nods, writes down a random price on an empty package for cinnamon and goes on with their chat.

2.17. Europe
16th century

2.18. Europe
16th–17th centuries

2.19. Praeceptor stirrup
16th–17th centuries

Praeceptor stirrups look like regular stirrups, typical of the early 17th century, but it is necessary to know a few secrets. If you press in some places, lower some cleats, instead of regular patterns, the so-called seal of Metatron, the angel of the divine presence, the names of Galgaliel, Barachiel, Salathiel, will appear. Three angels. This is the most cabalistic sign, a symbol of all the heretical teachings including that of the Knight's Templar.

2.20. Europe
16th century

2.21. Europe
16th century

2.22. Europe
Middle of the 18th century.

Pair. AR. Bronze. Weight – 798 g. Soldered with silver. Width of footing — 100 mm. Width at the base of arches — 80 mm. Pattern — carving on copper. Gilt —3–5 percent. Gilt has been carefully scratched out.

Quite an amusing stirrup. The hoops bear the symbols of the two Freemason lodges: the Great Scottish one and, possibly, the Lodge of Sorrow. It is interesting that the arrangement of the symbols, the sequence of them (from the bottom up) adhere to a direct ascending line (rather than a stepped formation) from the skull to the all-seeing eye which shows that the owner of the stirrup had a very high grade of initiation. Another strange aspect is that there are no rituals or customs in the Lodge's Orders (statutes) which involve a horse, let alone a saddled horse. The display of the Masonic symbols, especially of this high grade of initiation, was totally unthinkable in the common circumstances. One can easily notice that the footboard is rubbed over as well as the fastening ring with the belt of stirrup strap which proves that the stirrup has already been in use.

The stirrup history: At the beginning of the 20th century the pair of stirrups was sold together with 47 other items belonging to the Great Scottish Lodge, including aprons, skulls set in silver and ritual compasses. In the twenties the Lodge's collection was broken and mostly destroyed. The stirrups happened to appear in Altay, where they had been used by local shepherds strictly for the purpose of riding while cattle grazing. The gilt is likely to have been rubbed off there. Then they were acquired quite by chance in 1996 as a free supplement to an Altay shepherd saddle dated around the 1950s.

2.23. Europe
18th century

2.24. Europe
18th century

2.25. France
18th century

CHAPTER 3
SPURS

Above all else, spurs, the pieces of iron attached to the boots, have long been canonized by mankind as the primary symbol of riding, as a sign of a rider's mastery, and as the first and most romantic token of belonging to the horse's world.

A spur cult has existed and continues to exist. (Pluvinel and Guérinière mandatorily hooked spurs to their jackboots.)

According to the old Haute École canons, they occasionally prick affectionately or stick a horse's side in order to make his movements more acute and excited, and in this way add a neural zest to the Haute École elements, which imparts, it is thought, a special chic and a certain aesthetic.

In point of fact, the spur, in its most noble variant, is little distinguished from the twig, it only suggests a degree of emotionalism to the horse and the need for fulfilling one or the other element. Nothing more. (I don't even want to talk about the degenerate use of spurs by sportsmen; it is ignorant, extremely brutal and thoughtless.)

I, too, once saw the spur as an indispensable, sacred thing, the holiness of which had been confirmed by centuries of riding practice, the more so because the number of corrections to a horse's movement during training of difficult elements or during their fulfillment is so great that it would be difficult to do without the spur.

To position the rump, assure high lifting of the legs, maintain the rhythm, and all at the same time, add some fire to the horse's movement using only the manipulation of one's own weight and a switch seems almost impossible.

But despite the sanctity and loftiness of the spur wearers' names, despite the absolute canonization of the spur in literature and art, it is a disgusting object, disgusting to the highest degree.

If one is to be completely honest, of course.

I have, true, always had the splendid excuse, that, because my horses work without bridles, bits, and halters, if I overdo it or am rude with the spur, they will tell me about it on the spot.

I had persuaded myself that my spurs were not really spurs at all.

Mine were small Portuguese les perons, effectively a Tom Thumb or European dressage spur which is attached without straps, and on which the shank is cut off and slightly rounded.

Tom Thumb spurs cannot be considered spurs when it comes down to it.

Their origin is funny.

The world history of the spur is generally not a rich one.

Only Sarmats claim originality in the design of spurs and, possibly, the Syanbi, Alans and Huns, following their example. Only, judging by the latest excavations of

Samartian burial sites, their spur was a wide bow with thorns and two shackles which were attached to the rider's shin with thorns on the inside. Such a spur "operated" constantly, every minute, as long as the rider was on the horse.

Of course, the small Samartian horses, burdened with the heaviest horned armor and heavy riders, eternally underfed, with legs that were fractured (which the arthritic and arthrosic joints of the horses from the Pazyryk burial site confirm) and with sore backs, required not only the sharpest, but also a steady painful stimulus in order to move.

Hence, the barbaric form of "permanent action" spur.

The Romans, Greeks, and Europeans before the 12th century knew well enough the traditional shape of the spur, more or less pointed, a bit shorter or a bit longer, with a larger or smaller rowel, but it was a common spur all the same with which, of course, one could make a lot of trouble, but not immediately.

In the work, "About Asiatic and African Horses" there also is evidence of Arabian spurs: "Likewise, even the spurs of these riders, which look larger than nails, are used by them with great inhumanity; and in Barbary one can see at a stable horses in such pitiful condition that their blood streams from their snouts and sides."

The Arabian spurs from my collection confirm the validity of this work which was published as "long ago" as 1824 (see photo 3.2).

* * *

The Crusaders brought the style for spurs with a goad in the form of a straight or crooked thorn 30–35 centimeters long from Palestine (see photos 3.1, 3.5).

Such a spur, which was used in Europe for many years, was still called "Arabian" for a very long time.

As did the Arabians, the knights made direct use of it.

Myths that they stabbed through a thick horse blanket with a similar spur are absolute rubbish. Not one horse blanket with holes from spurs or traces of spur have been preserved in any collection of hippic antiquities.

Moreover, if a thick quilted horse blanket was put onto a horse, then somewhat larger "window-like openings" would have remained beneath the spurs.

The side was stabbed, and it was stabbed very deeply, the blood on the horse's sides being a sign of a rider's bravery and daring.

With knighthood's absolute inability to control the horse, a similar spur at least solved the problem of how to break abruptly into a gallop, and, again, as in the Sarmatian variant, only it was able to force an overloaded and, as a rule, ill horse at least to move somehow.

The Haute École fathers at the end of the 16th and in the 17th century again affirmed the common spur as the only feasible one, not the "Arabian."

True, the rowel, a toothed wheel or wheels (they numbered as many as three per spur) was still rather large and sharp.

The Gothic European spur is a completely pathological and outrageous variant.

Besides this is a direct action spur!

The peculiarity of the medieval seat (legs firmly forward with firm support in the stirrup) in no way warranted such a length and sharpness of spurs, nor the capability of cutting into the horse's belly in any extreme situation, even against the rider's wishes. (The horse can fall down, the rider's leg can "slide" back and sideways upon colliding with another rider or a man on foot and the horse, finally, can jump over something, inevitably dislodging the rider's legs.)

This example of the spur is pathological in its brutality, but it was common in 13th–15th centuries. They loved to use it in combination with the "sweet" military curb-bit (the one with hooks on the mouthpiece). Such shameless lethality of the spur, and in particular that such a variant was widely adopted for combat, once more demonstrates that the medieval horse was, roughly speaking, "a horse for one battle," a valuable creature, but nonetheless less valuable than the one-time opportunity to win or run away.

In photo 3.1 we have a typical military spur with a thorn shank 8 cm long, made of steel and weighing 220 grams. The shank shows signs of having been deformed and straightened frequently. It has also been sharpened several times.

A cross section of the shank reveals a diamond shape. I would rather link the above deformation and straightening of the shank to fitting the spur to legs that were different in their length than to the consequences of stabs into a horse's flesh. But with laboratory analysis, we found tiny particles of blood from different horses close to the stem of the shank. The spur was worn on an armoured leg, which is proven by a slight deformation caused by metal rubbing against metal on the inner sides of the heel band. The heel bands were also bent and stretched in order to widen and narrow them, which loosened the fastening rivet, which was later replaced.

According to legend, which has no scientific basis so far, this spur belonged to Pignatelli (see photo 3.6). It is made of steel weighing 187 grams. It is and absolute rarity (AR).

I have great doubts about the heel band, which bears diamond-shaped decorations characteristic of the late Gothic period. The supposition that the shank was attached later to the older heel band has already been disproved.

The character of the pitting corrosion of the metals and the method of steel processing in the manufacture of the heel band and shank are identical.

This mysterious spur was intended to soften the impact to the highest degree. The ends of the rowels have been rounded; the axle of the rowel ensures free rotation and a softer impact.

This type of spur (see photo 3.8) had been in fashion for rather a long period of time. The elaborate, multi-roweled spurs were a compulsory attribute of the "School masters" until the death of Louis XIV. The is the first published photograph of this absolute rarity. These bronze, steel and gilt spurs weigh 280 grams and have a total length of 21 cm.

The fastening chains haven't survived to the present day.

The gilt has been partially worn off. It has been better preserved on the "right" (outer) side of the heel band.

This enables us to make a bold conclusion that this is definitely the spur worn on the right heel. The design does not show other evidence of the spur being made to wear on the right or left heel.

The rivet fastening of the shank to the heel band is original.

The Haute École spur employs a completely different principle and, in comparison with the Gothic spur, the spur of the Huns, and the Mexican and German spurs, it is, in general, an example of delicacy and gentleness.

3.1. Gothic knight spur
13th–14th centuries

3.2. Europe
11th–15th centuries

3.3. Europe
17th century

3.4. Peru
17th century

3.5. Europe
15th century

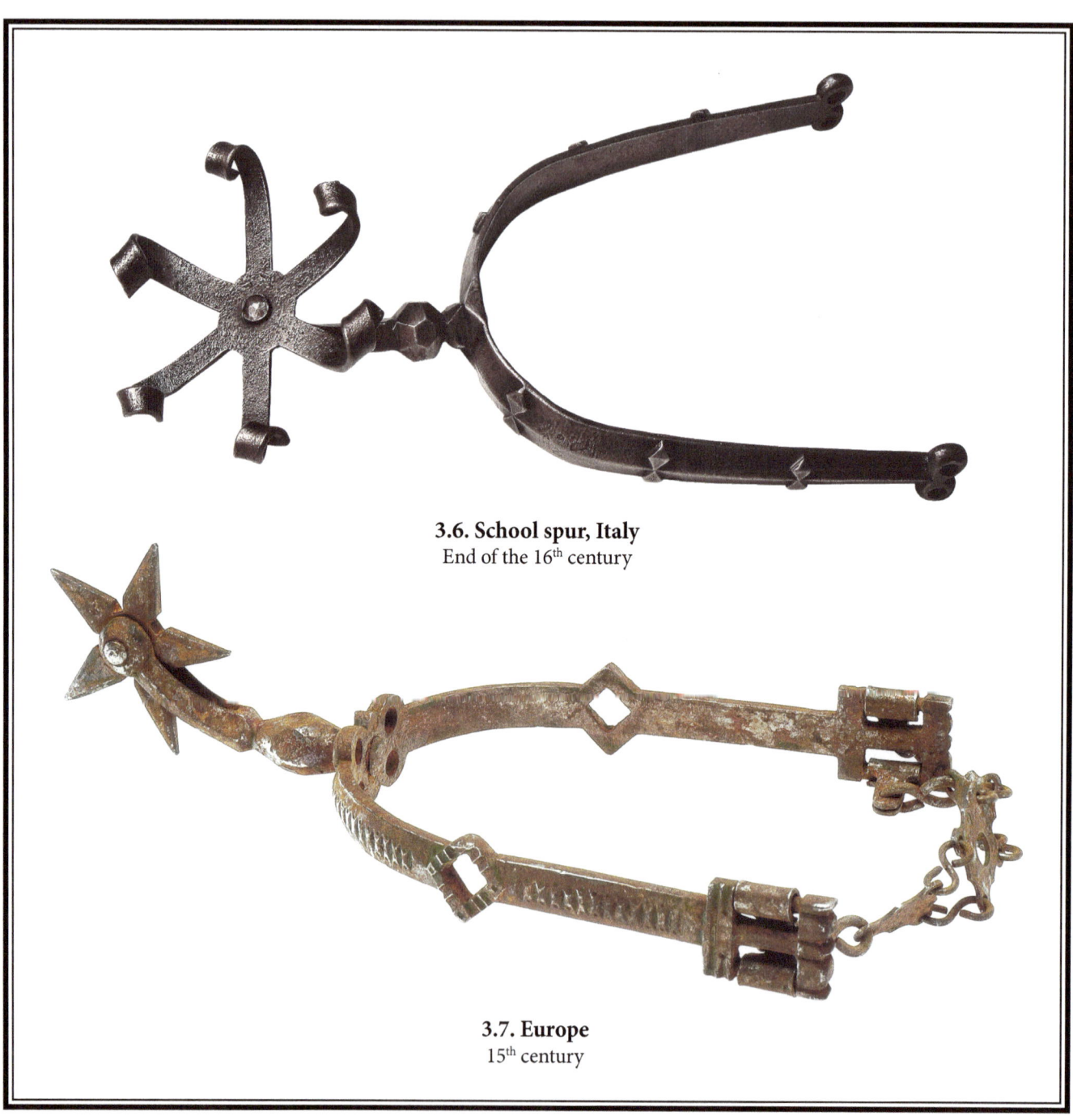

3.6. School spur, Italy
End of the 16th century

3.7. Europe
15th century

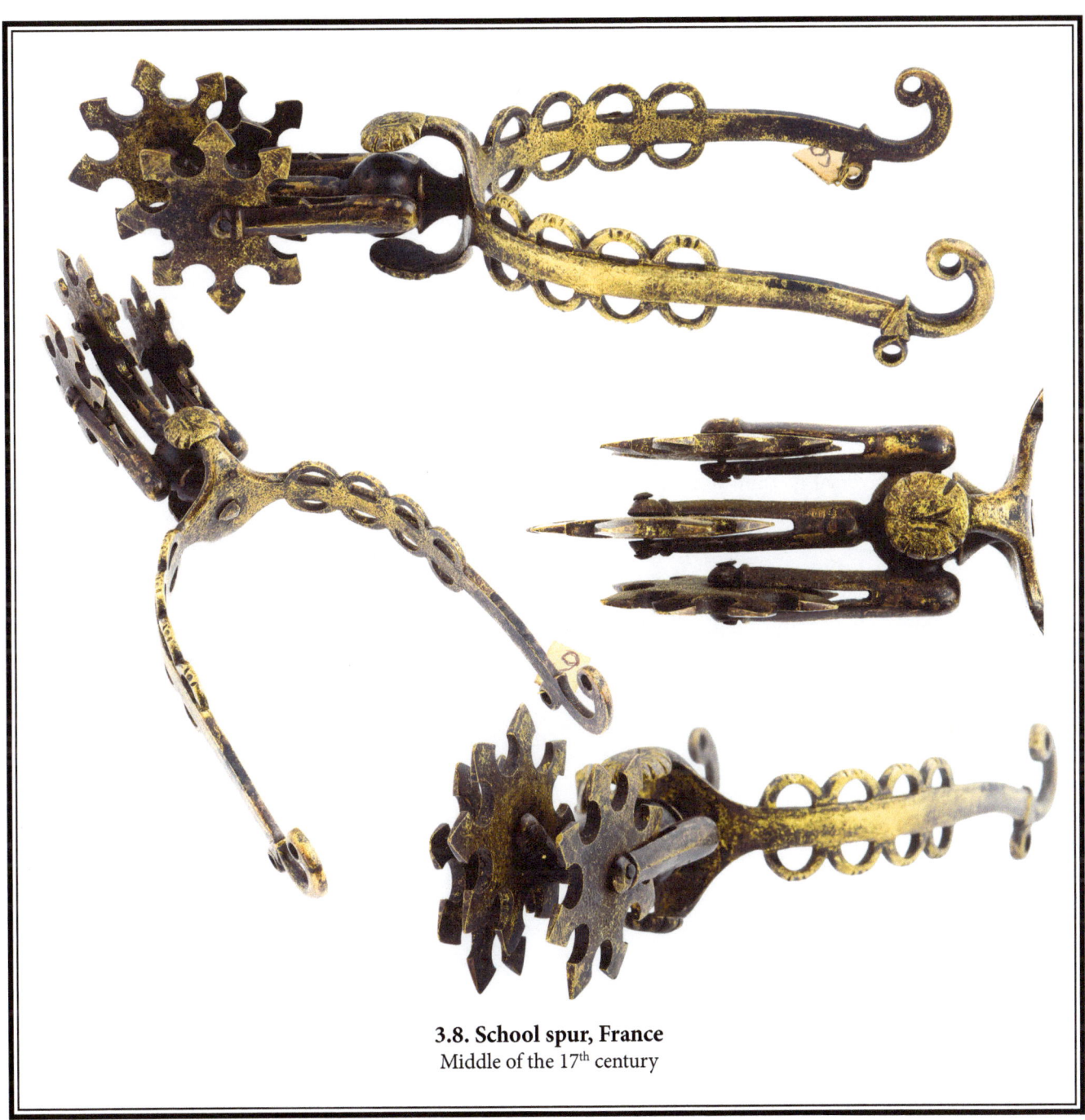

3.8. School spur, France
Middle of the 17th century

IRON

* * *

The cavalry of the 17th to 19th centuries, which did not require either skill or high school figures from a rider, or a special speed, overly simplified the spurs, shortening their goads, having reduced the rowels (the wheel itself) somewhat.

Particularly in such a form spurs became an indispensable part of the military uniform.

But at balls, gallant officers with sharp toothed rowels contrived to slash the skirts of the ladies while dancing in such a way that the latter resolved to give up dancing, which they announced through their tears.

Depriving the cavalry of dances was the deprivation of any desire to continue living.

The dance, as a universal method of flirtation, was an obligatory and unavoidable prologue to the feather bed or hayloft.

The choice was distressing.

It was either barracks homosexuality and goats, but in spurs, or traditional delightful sexual banditry, but without the spurs. In practice homosexuality and goats turned out to be more terrible, and ultimately inspired the officers to remove the toothed rowel and contrive for the ballroom a certain decorative variety of spur, the so-called Tom Thumb, which was safe for skirts. In this way the presence of some kind of iron pieces on the feet, which were mandatory in uniform, was complied with, and the skirts remained intact.

The dances continued, to the satisfaction of one and all.

Thousands of discarded goats throughout Europe suffered terribly for a time, but afterwards returned to fulfilling their routine goat obligations, only sometimes allowing themselves a melancholy chorus of bleating after the departing troops.

In Tom Thumb spurs, which returned European officers to a normal sex life, there was one colossal deficiency: they did not jingle like real spurs.

People wrestled with this "problem" for a couple of decades, introducing into the hollow shank of the Tom Thumb spur different balls and bells, but then they shrugged it off and forgot about it, and the Tom Thumb spur, the ballroom spur, remained as we see it now: safe for skirts, but, nonetheless, to a great degree unhealthy for the sides and stomach of the horse.

3.9. Europe
18th century

3.10. Ottoman spur, Algeria
Second half of the 20th century
Silver inlay with engraved racemes and coral; length: 31 centimeters

3.11. Germany
16th century

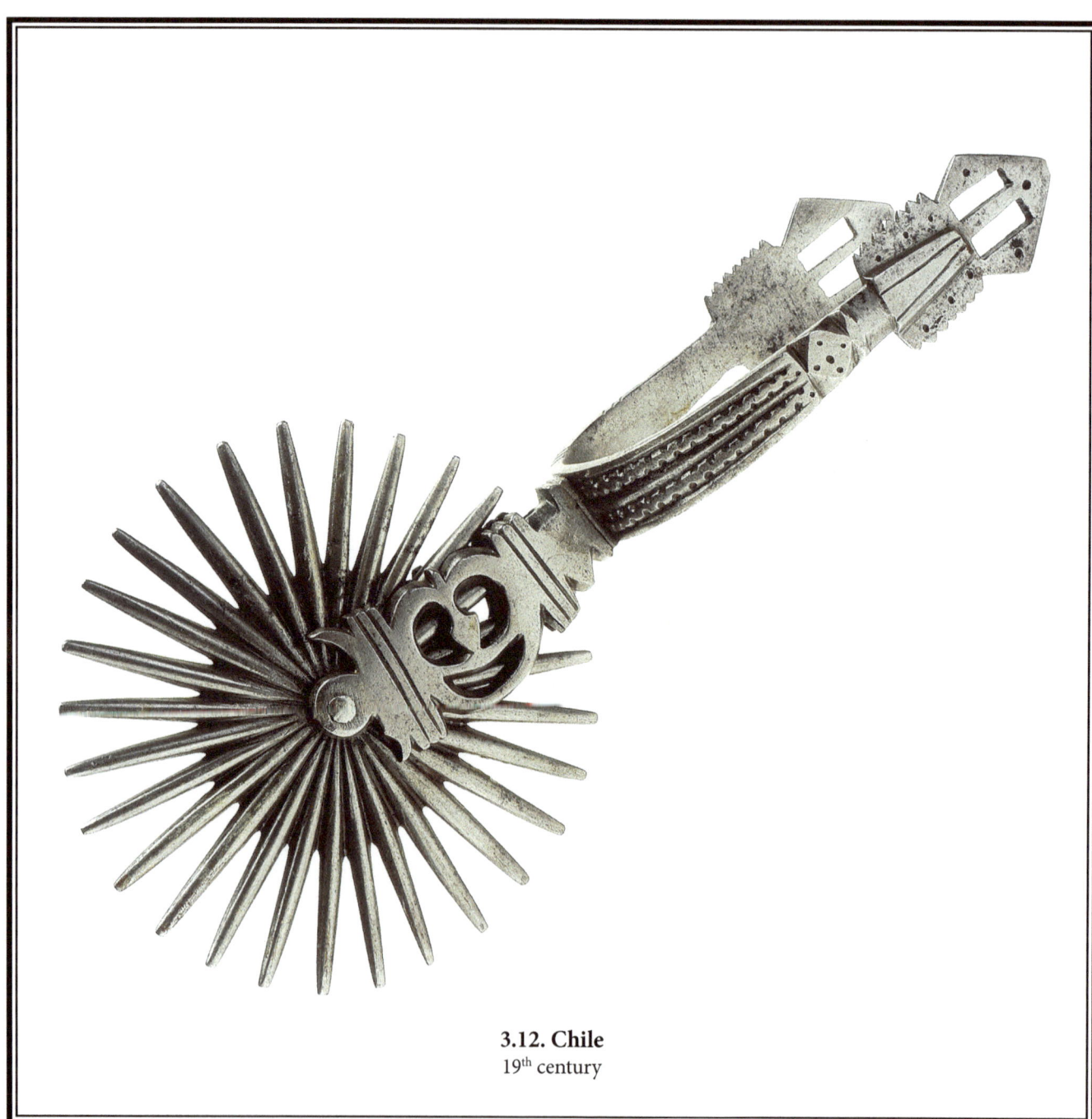

3.12. Chile
19th century

CHAPTER 4
HORSE ARMOR AND ESPINAS (CALTROPS)

Armor for horses also is a myth.

It is possible to put as much iron as one likes onto a horse, but it is impossible to protect its most fragile parts, its legs, while not paralyzing the horse's motor functions completely.

And in reality the horse's legs are strikingly fragile.

Almost any injury to the legs has major consequences for the horse. Any blow, whether with a stone, stick, axe or a shield would make the horse instantly lame and unsuitable for further combat.

In the Battle of Legnica (1241), when Batu's Mongols met face-to-face with Western European knights, the Mongols purposefully and uniformly destroyed the knights' horses in particular, hacking off and firing at their legs. It wasn't difficult for them from their short horses (nearly 120–125 centimeters high to the withers). The Mongolian bowmen at Legnica virtually didn't fire at the knights themselves or the protected chests of the horses.

Organized, precise and with fiendish accuracy, they fired at the horses legs, piercing the carpus and fetlock. (The carpus or fetlock, or the horse's hock are a rather large target for a good shot from a bow).

Grand Duke Henry II the Pious of Poland and Silesia perished in approximately the same way — the Mongols pierced all four legs of his mount, and then they beat Henry the Pious with bludgeons and hatchets.

Then the whole thing ended, by the way, with the Mongols' complete victory, as did all other clashes with heavy knight elements.

The Mongols knew better than anyone how to be merciless when it came to horses and possibly knew better than their enemies how to kill horses quickly and in huge numbers. (They had colossal experience in this matter, for the Mongols grew up only on horse meat and actually were brought up with horse blood which they drank in great quantity and with much satisfaction.)

Horse armor in no way hindered those massive horse massacres which the Mongols arranged both outside Legnica and near Sandomir, and in all the battles of the "Magyar" and "Polish" campaigns.

I had occasion to examine thoroughly the real fighting armor of European horses.

For hours, and very closely.

Only at Warwick Castle in England was I able to find on an armor crupper something looking like the marks of blows from a halberd or a large lance. But all the other horse armor does not have any combat perforations on its upper part.

The strike of a crossbow's "bolt" or a long arrow from a heavy bow leaves a very characteristic mark on any medieval armor, both a man's and a horse's.

There are hardly any of them on any piece of horse armor.

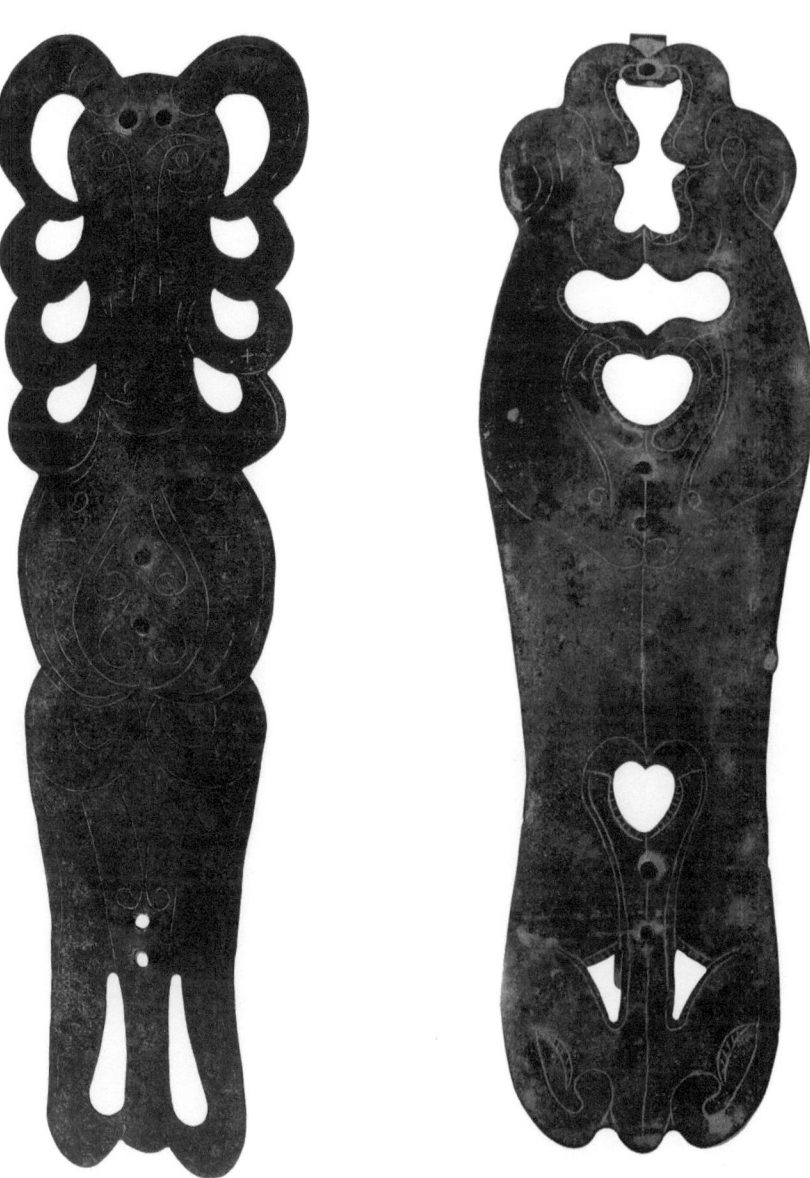

4.1. Shaffrons (faceplates) from the ornate bridles from Scythian Tombs
4th century B.C.

4.2. Scythian bridle ornament
4th century B.C.

4.3. Shaffron, Europe
17th century

4.4. Indo Persian Shaffron with three horns
India, circa 18th century

This shaffron has eight unusual figures, a pair of each figure, one on each side of helmet. They are hand carved astonishing figures like horse and man, flying horse, man and horse flying. There is brass decoration all over with fine engraving of flower motifs. Made of heavy steel it is hammered and chiseled by hand. It measures about 27" high.

4.5. Indo Persian Shaffron with ten spikes
India, circa 18th century

Brass decoration all over with fine engraving of flower motifs. Made of heavy steel, hammered and chiseled by hand. It measures about 30" high.

I am not talking about parade, ceremonial, gilded or inlaid shaffrons, cruppers or peytrels.

I have in mind the relatively simple combat armor which was, by all indications, in frequent usage.

By "all indications," I mean the presence of an old horse hair on the inside face, where the armor "joint" always and without fail rubbed the horse's skin.

By the way, judging by the abundance of these little hairs, which are removed easily from these joints with tweezers, there is the suspicion that often there was no horse blanket worn beneath the armor. Many horses bore this armor, since the tweezers retrieved strands of all colors from these joints and short summer strands as well as long winter hairs.

Gigantic depressions, which are created on the armor because a horse has fallen, and which was carefully straightened later, were noticed on much of the armor.

But there are hardly any signs either of arrow hits or direct blows with a sword or lance on this armor, despite the fact that they clearly were worn a lot and in very different circumstances. It is possible to conjecture precisely from all these objects that all the blows were addressed only to the legs, stomach and underside of the neck; that is, those places where in principle no armor can go.

The bas-reliefs of Trajan's Column preserve outright fantasy depictions of Sarmatian horses dressed in a certain "tricot" of scale armor. The whole horse, including the legs, hooves and nostrils, would have been covered, as if the armor was glued to the horse, armor which, ideally, was made of boiled and straightened horses' hooves.

If this were really the case, then the thickness of the horse's legs would have been doubled, owing to the thickness of the "armor" which had a certain base and backing of horny fragments. Under those circumstances, any bending of the legs would have been absolutely impossible.

Nevertheless, the immunity of Sarmatian horses, according to the evidence both of Arrian and Pausanias, was in reality very fundamental and exceeded everything imaginable — thus giving rise to the fantasy armor "tricot" on the bas-reliefs.

The fundamental nature of the scales that covered the upper neck, chest and croup totally did not interfere with the Roman infantrymen constantly beating the Sarmatian cavalry, which they did in Moesia (winter of 69), and during the Marcomannic Wars (173) and during the Roman-Dacian wars, when the Sarmatians were loyal allies of the Dacian king Decebalus.

* * *

We can't not mention the existence of the "caltrop" and all the other hazardous devices deliberately planted to injure cavalry horses. All peoples at all times made use of these devices which made any attack by cavalry both senseless and disastrous for the attackers. The fields of large clashes, where an attack of enemy cavalry was expected (in accordance with the terrain or tactical situation), were seeded with these caltrops as thickly as possible. A multitude of diversions and maneuvers existed, the purpose of which was to scatter as many caltrops as possible in places where enemy horses might be.

They were used everywhere.

Any museum of a historic collection, even the poorest, counts hundreds of such caltrops of very different types. With hooks on the ends of the thorns and without hooks,

4.6. Espina (tribula or caltrop)
age unknown

with faceted stingers and flat. Such a phenomenal wealth of exhibits of this type is connected with the fact that very many of them have been preserved, they are very cheap and they find very many of them in excavations and when plowing fields.

I discovered a full box (about 15 kilograms) of Swedish, Dutch, Russian and German caltrops in the Arsenal files of the Knight's Hall at the Hermitage. Even I was not able to precisely attribute all of them to their "nationality," inasmuch as the caltrop was an international, ubiquitous, conventional thing.

It is a very cunning device (see photo 4.6). When it is thrown, it always lands with the sharp end upwards and is absolutely stable on any ground. And it is perfectly unnoticeable in grass, sand and even in mud.

A horse cut on a caltrop receives a terribly intense and deep puncture of the hoof. The sting of a caltrop passes through the horny sole of the hoof to the deep flexor tendon and to the navicular and coffin bones.

A horse, continuing its movement ahead through inertia, drives the caltrop ever deeper into the leg, turns it over there and converts the hoof into a bloody mass.

A wound like this was always fatal for the horse in the conditions of a lack of antiseptics and anti-tetanus vaccine.

The inability take a step on the affected leg and the terrible painful shock made the horse so lame that it was impossible to force it to move even with beatings.

Caltrops were known in Assyria, Scythia, medieval Europe, in Asia, and later, everywhere and during all eras.

The fates of cavalry attacks were not decided by archers and arbalesters nor bullets and grapeshot. Although they threw everything primarily at the horses, for they were larger and easier targets, their fates were decided by those small caltrops which were sown in the battlefields and engagement sites.

Everyone, in every army of the world and at all times, knew about the caltrops, about the fact that they could be everywhere, and that getting one of them into a horse's foot was the death of it. And a cavalry flying recklessly at full tilt at an enemy is a cinematic pack of lies and nothing more.

(By the way, that freedom with which the conquistadors at first made mincemeat of the Aztecs, that effectiveness of a direct equestrian attack which so astounded their enemies, was connected most of all with the fact that caltrops were completely unknown to Montezuma's warriors. They were, obviously, the only people of the world who did not know them for a long while. By as early as Pizarro's time, the caltrops would appear even here.)

4.7. Pendants for the bags of horse doctors
Far North, Russia, 16th–18th centuries

ABOUT THE COLLECTION

The desire to ornament a horse somehow lives inside every horse person, or so it seems. Why else would they ever invent all that splendor?

Well known Russian film director, journalist, politician, scientist and writer Alexander Nevzorov, who is virtually a Spartan, was also charmed by those intricate things.

His interest in horse iron arose naturally in parallel to his interest in the old classical Haute École, in which entourage is of a great importance.

One of the main attributes of the Haute École is, of course, beautiful bits. We've always wanted to move away from the esthetics of equestrian sports and we've invented a lot of ways to do so. We ordered special, Haute École-styled saddles for which they made us custom stirrups which were "soft" (without any edges that could work as a spur) but "ornate" in Pluvinel's epoch style.

They were successful experiments, but later we began to collect some real specimens.

This book does not present the whole NHE collection but merely a part of it. Although, this part is the most distinctive one. Even so, Alexander Nevzorov is not prone to call his conglomerate of horse iron "a collection" and holds no reverence towards it.

The collection (let us call it this, after all) started with some simple curb bit bought at Portobello Road in London. Actually we bought it for its intended usage, i.e. — to ride a horse with the help of it. But we soon found out that this curb bit was completely useless because it fell apart before we could actually use it. Thus it came to rest on some nail on a wall in our house.

Almost all the specimens (not including the ones which can cause severe pain in a horse) were worn by a horse for at least one time. A lot of those things were beautiful from an artistic point of view, but also were fiendish towards the horse and thus could not be used. They were dismantled and ruthlessly modernized.

We welded modern, "softer" mouthpieces in the ancient curb bits. We've attached Scythian cheek pieces to the halters so they would look "nice" and there would be no bit in the horse's mouth.

In the end, when we realized completely that there are NO bits which can be used to ride a horse, these mountains of broken, re-made and re-welded things were stuffed into the chests and attics like some treasures for our future great-grandchildren.

Many pieces which were not modernized in any way because they are extremely, villainously cruel to the horse are of a great interest for everyone who studies hippology; for the ones who really want to know the history of horsemanship; for the ones who are strong enough to understand the true essence of human-horse relationships and to deny the hippological heritage of the use of all those bits in the relationship with a horse.

With visionary inspiration Alexander founded the School of Nevzorov Haute École (NHE) which evolved quickly to where, in only five years from its inception, he had not only stopped using any bits, but also stopped any mounted work with horses — principles fully embraced by the many NHE School students today. Along the way he produced powerful films, wrote epochal books and hundreds of articles.

It can be said that this collection of antique iron played a great role in forming his view toward horsemanship. It was the starting point of a hippological education. It helped uncover the truth of which everyone was silent for hundreds of years.

Nevzorov's interests have surpassed equine iron by now, though we still have this beautiful collection that continues to serve well anyone who wishes to study the history of the relationship between a horse and a human.

Lydia Nevzorova

CONTENTS

Preface
3
Introduction
5
Chapter 1. Bits
7
Chapter 2. Stirrups
81
Chapter 3. Spurs
115
Chapter 4. Horse Armor and Espinas (Caltrops)
129
About the Collection
140

www.ingramcontent.com/pod-product-compliance
Lightning Source LLC
Chambersburg PA
CBHW041510220426
43661CB00047B/1527